THE QUICK AND EASY GUIDE

TO

Compass
Correction

By the same author:

Boatmen's Guide to Light Salvage

Knight's Modern Seamanship,
17th & 18th editions (contributor)

Primer of Towing

Revised Primer of Towing

Shiphandling with Tugs

Marine Salvage*

*also published by Sheridan House

THE QUICK AND EASY GUIDE

TO

Compass
Correction

GEORGE H. REID

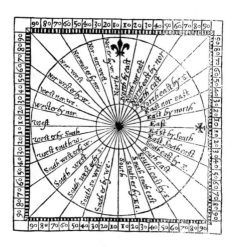

SHERIDAN HOUSE

First published 1997 by
Sheridan House Inc.
145 Palisade Street
Dobbs Ferry, NY 10522

The purchaser is encouraged to photocopy and enlarge the Compass
Correction Chart and Skyclock for personal use.

Library of Congress Cataloging-in-Publication Data

Reid, George H., 1924–
    The quick and easy guide to compass correction / George H. Reid.
        p.   cm.
    Includes index.
    ISBN 1-57409-023-2 (alk. paper)
    1. Compass.   I. Title.
    VK577.R45   1997
    623.89'2—dc21   97-24701
                                                                            CIP

Illustrations by Camilla Reid
Design by Jeremiah B. Lighter

Printed in the United States of America

ISBN 1-57409-023-2

*This volume is dedicated to
Ginny,
my favorite mentor*

Contents

Preface   1

1

An Introduction to Compass Error

3

2

The Magnetic Compass: How it Works

7

3

Compass Error and Its Causes

9

4

Applying Compass Error

15

5

How to Find Compass Error

19

6

An Explanation of Compass Correction Tables
23

7

Swinging Ship: How to Set Up a Deviation Table
31

8

Adjusting the Compass
35

9

Summary
41

10

Sources of Nautical Books, Charts, and Navigational Instruments
45

Appendices
49

Index
65

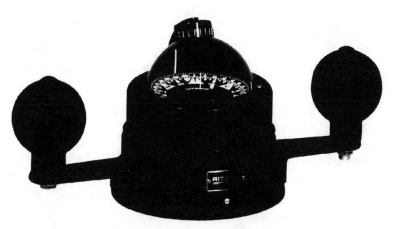

This special shock mounted binnacle compass
features quadrantal spheres for steel boat installation.
Courtesy E.S. Ritchie & Sons, Inc.

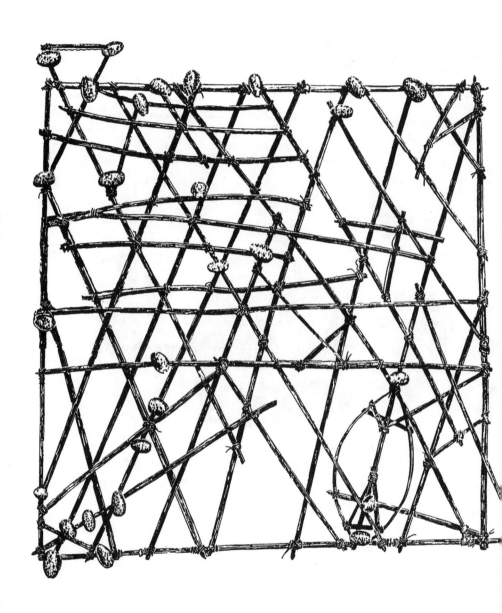

A woven Micronesian chart

Preface

A FRIEND OF MINE from the Paradise Bar has an interesting memento of his years in the Pacific. It is an irregularly woven piece of latticework with cowrie shells lashed at seemingly random intervals on a grid made of sticks from pandanus and palms.

If you are mystified as to its purpose, you share illustrious company; so was Captain James Cook, the redoubtable explorer.

The object is a chart of the type constructed by the navigators of Polynesia and Micronesia as a reference for their often extended voyages between the islands. In the distant past, the voyagers of Oceania had no compasses to guide them, so they were obliged to rely upon their knowledge of the wind, the sea, and the sky to plot their courses. In this case the art of navigation was clearly distinguished from the science.

Even in our enlightened age, some of the old arts persist, but only a few of us have either the experience or the perception to rely upon them completely.

Nevertheless, there is a common ground shared by both art and science that a boater might find of interest. Perhaps the information contained in this text will lead to some understanding and appreciation of those skills that are part of the sailor's art.

1

✳

An Introduction to Compass Error

APTAIN AHAB, master of the whaler *Pequod,* had other problems beside his nemesis, the great white whale. In chapter 24 of *Moby Dick* the reader finds that the square-rigger's compass magnets have had their polarity reversed by lightning during a thunderstorm. Fortunately, the clever Ahab understands what has happened and remedies his problem with a magnetized sail needle, using it to replace the inverted magnets.

Recently a cruising yacht reported a similar incident after crossing the equator. The manufacturer of the compass attributed this strange reversal of polarity to the change in hemispheres. There is no evidence to support this conclusion, and no authoritative text indicates that this theory is plausible. The reversal of the compass' polarity was probably caused by internal or external electrical forces. High-voltage electric lines can also be a factor as discussed later in this chapter.

I first became shipmate with magnetic compasses when I started going to sea as a teenager during the early 1940s. At first I served as a seaman and helmsman, and later as a ship's officer.

These were troubled times during World War II. The ships, mostly freighters and tankers with some troopships thrown in, usually traveled in convoy in the war zones. Only a few of them were equipped with gyro compasses, and the rest were dependent upon conventional magnetic compasses for the courses that were steered.

Compass error was a critical factor at this time. None of the merchant vessels had radar, which was still in its infancy. A mistake in a vessel's course during heavy fog or a period of restricted visibility in a convoy numbering up to a hundred ships could, and did, cause collisions - often with serious results.

My first experience with unexpected compass error occurred after the Allied invasion of France during the war. I was third mate on a Liberty ship bound up the English Channel from Cherbourg to Boulogne-sur-Mer. I had relieved the chief mate who had just altered the ship's course into a narrow unmarked channel which had been swept free of mines. Automatically taking an azimuth of the sun, I found a gross error in the compass' new and supposedly true course that was posted on the blackboard. I advised my superiors, but both the captain and the chief mate scoffed at my findings.

But, hanging tough, I took another azimuth which confirmed my first results. Then I noticed the culprit. Someone, presumably my predecessor on the watch, had left the "loud hailer" (a hand-held, battery-powered voice amplifier) near the binnacle. Its strong magnetic field had affected the compass.

There was an embarrassed silence from my senior officers when I removed the offending instrument from its location near the compass. Had it remained undisturbed in its original location, there might have been some interesting results. The ship's cargo included 3,000 tons of high explosives, and there were active mines in the adjacent waters. This was a valuable lesson.

Ships in those days went to considerable effort to determine their deviation and compass error. They were regularly "swung," and had their compasses adjusted. Azimuths were taken on every watch and at every change of course to determine compass error, if visibility permitted. Freighters even tried to keep their booms stowed in the same position to maintain the compass deviation unchanged.

Today, practices of this kind are generally overlooked on most modern ships since they are equipped with gyro compasses. This also accounts for some accidents that have occurred when vessels are stranded as a result of gyro failure - and the failure of the vessel's bridge watch to verify the gyro's error.

But deepwater ships are not the only vessels where compass error should be known. Anyone who ventures offshore should know his vessel's compass error, and how to find it. Thanks to a schooner captain I knew, I devised a simple method that provides this information. He had to deliver an expensive yacht from Puerto Rico to Jamaica. Since this was before Global Positioning System (GPS) became available, and he was not a navigator, he depended upon dead reckoning to determine his position. He naturally wanted to know how to check his compass error when he was at sea. *Voilà,* the answer was easy: amplitudes. The sun's amplitude is its bearing when rising or setting. Those that I calculated for his voyage remained unchanged from his departure to his arrival, and provided him with a convenient means of checking his compass error twice a day. This occasion gave me the idea of developing the table of amplitudes included in this text.

This same table of amplitudes later helped in the "recovery" of a tug and barge that had somehow disappeared in the Caribbean and wound up in Barranquilla, Colombia. The tug had lain at a berth in a shipyard near a high-voltage power line, and, like the *Pequod,* its compass had been seriously affected. Thanks to the amplitude tables, the vessel's compass error was duly noted, and it was delivered to a safe port without going aground on an isolated reef or missing its landfall.

2

✳

The Magnetic Compass: How It Works

A FEW YEARS ago my daughter's teacher asked me to demonstrate to a classroom full of fifth grade students how a magnetic compass works. So, like Captain Ahab, I magnetized a needle, stuck it into a broom straw, and floated this arrangement in a cup of water. I compared its direction with the north head of the card in a lifeboat compass, brought along as an example. Both of them were in perfect alignment. Whenever the needle was deflected, it returned unfailingly and pointed towards magnetic north again.

This session was mutually enlightening, and I had demonstrated the principle of one of the oldest instruments used in navigation.

No one knows for certain when or where the magnetic compass first came into use. There are various theories. One of these attributes the discovery of its use in Asia to Marco Polo. However, other sources indicate that such compasses were already in use in the Mediterranean at this time. The Norsemen were certainly familiar with the compass by the eleventh century. Given the extent of their voyages to Greenland, Iceland, and North America, it seems likely that they had some knowledge of it before that.

Whatever the facts may be regarding the origin of the magnetic compass, the principle remains the same. Magnetized iron rods or needles are attached to a compass card and suspended so they are free to pivot in a horizontal plane and align themselves with the magnetic meridian. The compass card that the magnets are attached to predates the compass, for it was derived from the wind rose of the ancients.

The magnets, of course, are simply reacting to the magnetic properties of the earth itself. The *red* end of the magnet in the compass is attracted to the earth's north magnetic pole (the *blue* pole). The *blue* end of the compass magnet is repulsed by the earth's *blue* pole and is attracted by the earth's *red* or south magnetic pole. The magnets, supposedly, respond like affairs of the heart: like repels like and opposites attract.

3

✳

Compass Error
and Its Causes

ANY VESSEL that goes offshore should have a compass, unless it happens to have a woven Micronesian chart and someone on board who knows how to use it. It is also a good idea to have a compass aboard boats in inshore waters where fog or reduced visibility can be expected. However, a compass is only useful to you if you know how much *error* it has, and you know how to apply the *correction* in order to determine the true compass courses or bearings.

Compass error is defined as the angular difference between true north and compass north. It is
also the algebraic sum of *deviation* and *variation*,
the forces that cause the deflection of the compass'
head from true north. These forces are named E or W
to indicate the direction of their effect. Like names
(E or W) are added, and in the case of unlike names,
the smaller is subtracted from the larger.

If the compass is mounted on a wooden or fiber-
glass boat remote from the instrument panel, electronic equipment, or any fixtures made of iron or
steel, it is probable that the only error will be caused
by variation.

Variation is defined as the angular difference
between the magnetic meridian and the geographic
meridian. It is constant on all headings at a given
location. This results in part from the fact that the
positions of the magnetic poles do not conform to
those of the geographic poles (Fig. 1). Variation is
indicated on the compass roses of nautical charts.
On many large-scale charts and pilot charts, it is
also indicated by lines of magnetic variation. But
take care: variation is subject to change. This annual increase or decrease is indicated on the compass rose (Fig. 2). Be sure to check the date on your
charts.

Deviation is the angular difference between
compass north and magnetic north. This error results from magnetic forces aboard the vessel itself
that deflect the compass heading from the correct
magnetic heading. Errors caused by deviation are

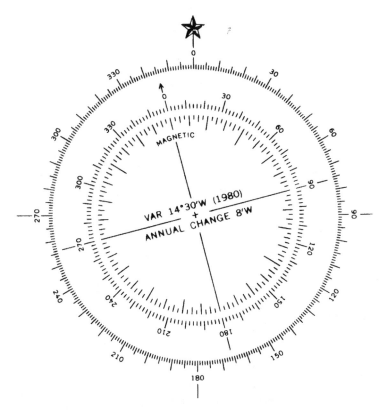

Fig. 1. Compass rose showing variation and annual change.
Courtesy DMAHTC Pub. 226

not constant, but change from heading to heading. For this reason it is wise to prepare a Compass Deviation Card that shows the amount of deviation on headings 15 to 30 degrees apart.

Misalignment is an error caused by the lubber's line being improperly lined up. This is most often found if the compass is located away from the vessel's centerline, usually for the helmsman's conve-

• 11 •

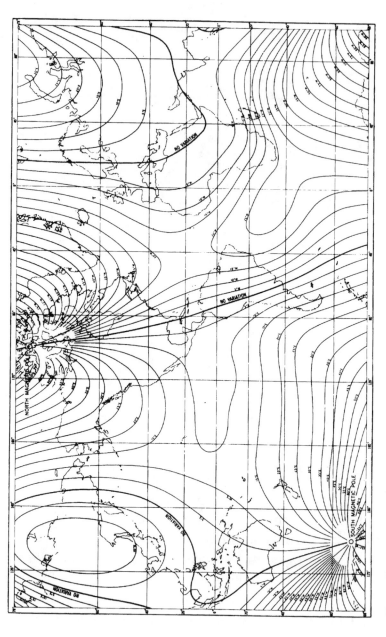

Fig. 2. Earth's magnetic variation chart. *Courtesy DMAHTC Pub. 226*

nience. This error is constant on all headings and can be removed by properly aligning the compass.

Lazy Compass is a compass that either moves very slowly or not at all when the vessel makes a large change of course. This can be attributed to a number of causes:

Mechanical Wear

The jeweled bearing in the compass card that rides on the pivot point gets a lot of wear from the constant oscillation of the compass. It is not unusual for it to suffer damage from this, especially in high-speed boats or those with a lively motion. The friction from this wear and tear can impede the motion of the card.

Weak Magnets

These are fairly common in older compasses, particularly if the vessel has been laid up for a long time. In some instances they may become completely demagnetized. This may also result from the effects of heavy electrical cables that are located in the vicinity of where the vessel is docked or secured.

Frozen Compass is a compass that is locked on one heading regardless of how the vessel is turned. It seems to occur only on steel vessels, usually if the compass is close to one of the bulkheads rather than centrally located. Some surplus military craft have wheelhouses constructed of armor steel which is heavily magnetic. This can have a very noticeable effect on the compass. If this condition is difficult to correct with compensating magnets, it may be necessary to install a remote-reading compass with a repeater in the wheelhouse to steer by.

In any case, if the compass is "lazy" or "frozen," it should be removed from the boat to an area free of magnetic forces and turned rapidly in different directions several times. If the compass card is lively and returns quickly to a proper heading without oscillating, the problem stems from its location. However, if it is lazy or hesitant in returning to its heading, the problem is probably mechanical. If the card pivots freely but slowly and swings back and forth before settling down, the problem is probably caused by weak magnets.

Intermittent Deviation is often caused by the compass being located too close to electrical or electronic equipment. Even the electric wires that supply the electricity to the compass light can deflect the compass, if it is direct current, which is commonly used on small boats. If that is the case, the cord should be twisted to avoid affecting the compass. To check for this kind of error, operate the equipment when the boat is secured alongside a dock on a constant heading, and see if the compass is deflected when the electrical current is turned on.

4

✳

Applying
Compass Error

A FEW YEARS ago, a crusty old charterboat captain I knew set out on a voyage from Miami to Bimini. His landfall was embarrassingly far from his destination, and his return trip left no doubt that he was off the mark by a wide margin.

When I saw him, he had his compass under his arm and was muttering about "taking this damn compass ashore to get it corrected." I stopped him before he got off the dock, and found (as I suspected) that his compass was mounted on the flying bridge near the electric tachometers on the engine panel. It was also close to the radiotelephone and the recording depth finder.

I explained the facts of life to him and told him that his problem was on board his boat. But he still wouldn't believe me until he checked with one of the local compass adjusters. He never thanked me, but I got a lot of dolphin fillets after that.

The term "correcting the compass" is ambiguous. Some people assume it to mean the same thing as adjusting the compass or reducing compass deviation. It doesn't. It simply means applying the known compass error to the *compass course* in order to find the *true course*; conversely, the term "uncorrecting the compass" means applying the *compass error* to the *true course* to find the *compass course* for a given heading. In order to do this, you must know how the error is named (E or W) and how to apply it.

It's easy. If compass north lies to the right of true north, the error is easterly. If the compass north lies to the left of true north, the compass error is westerly.

In correcting the compass, that is, converting the compass heading to the true heading, westerly deviation or variation is subtracted, and easterly variation or deviation is added.

In uncorrecting the compass, which means converting the true course to the compass course to be steered, the process is reversed.

It may be easier to remember the order in which this is done by memorizing the two old saws shown below in the left-hand column:

CORRECTING	(EAST +	WEST -)
CAN	Compass heading	120°
DEAD	Deviation	-8°W
MEN	Magnetic Heading	112°
VOTE	Variation	+3°E
TWICE	True Heading	115°

UNCORRECTING	(EAST -	WEST +)
TIMID	True Heading	261°
VIRGINS	Variation	- 6°E
MAKE	Magnetic heading	255°
DULL	Deviation	+3°W
COMPANIONS	Compass Heading	258°

For my own part it has proven less confusing simply to remember "Compass To True - Add East And Subtract West." Figure 3 shows the relationship between true, magnetic, and compass headings.

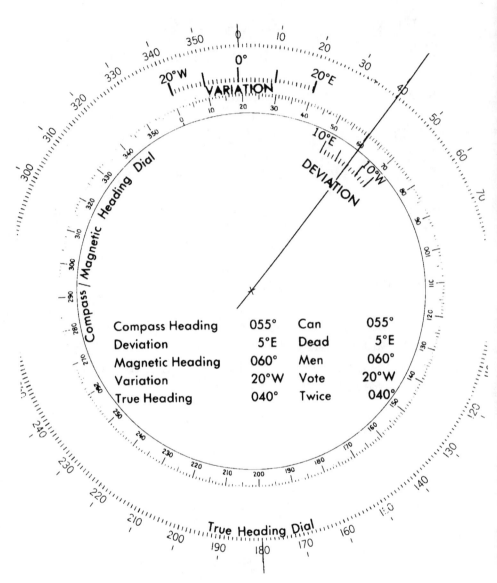

Compass Heading	055°	Can	055°
Deviation	5°E	Dead	5°E
Magnetic Heading	060°	Men	060°
Variation	20°W	Vote	20°W
True Heading	040°	Twice	040°

Fig. 3. Relationships between variation, deviation and headings.
Courtesy DMAHTC Pub. 226

• 18 •

5

*

How to Find
Compass Error

THERE ARE better ways to find your compass error than by missing your projected landfall by a conspicuous distance - especially when you have some paying customers on board. This usually involves taking bearings. Now for some reason, taking bearings is not always easy on small boats. I suppose that some boat builders assume that compasses are only for steering and overlook the fact that they are useful for plotting the boat's position by taking compass bearings.

If the compass is either a standard Navy or spherical type with the lubber's line forward, and if the view is unimpeded, good bearings can usually be taken by sighting down a straightedge or parallel ruler laid over the center of the compass card.

However, if the view is restricted or if the compass is of the direct reading type, it may be necessary to construct a pelorus or "dummy compass." This is easy. You simply paste a compass rose from an old chart or a plotting sheet onto a square of corrugated box material, plywood, or stiff cardboard. It is also handy to affix a wood or plastic sight vane to it that pivots about the center of the card.

The reason that a square piece of cardboard or plywood is suggested is that this can often be aligned by pressing one edge against a wheelhouse window - fore and aft or athwartship - so long as it is square or parallel to the vessel's centerline. The paper pelorus can also be taped to the deck or cabin top if it's more convenient. The boat should be level when bearings are taken this way, as this rig is not gimbaled. The bearings are normally *relative* and must be added to or subtracted from the boat's compass heading.

The next question is: If the bearings are taken for the purpose of determining compass error, what should the bearings be taken from? That depends. In inland waters harbor charts often have ranges (two markers in a line) that indicate the center of a channel. This is a handy reference commonly used by compass adjusters. A boat operator can check the compass error on as many headings as he wants as the boat crosses the ranges. Prominent structures are plotted on charts; a line drawn through them can provide another source of bearings. Quite frequently, structures like docks and piers are constructed on east-west or north-south headings. When this is the case, they can also be used as references for correcting a boat's compass.

Offshore you can take bearings of a distant object from a known position, for example, a lighthouse from a sea buoy six to eight miles away. The position of radio towers, prominent buildings, water tanks, and other structures is usually shown on charts; these can also be used as ranges. Even landmarks like capes that fall in line can provide an accurate range. You may have to look about a bit, but there is nearly always something handy that can be used for this purpose.

On the high seas, you must rely upon bearings of a celestial body like the sun, the moon, the stars, or planets. In order to do this, you must be able to determine the true bearing of the object observed.

This is easy to do if you have an accurate time-piece, a *Nautical Almanac,* a set of "Red" *Azimuth Tables, Publication 260,* navigation tables like *Publication 229* or *Publication 249* - and know how to use them. But even if you don't, there are still ways to determine your compass error.

In the northern hemisphere you can take bearings of the North Star, Polaris. Even with uncorrected bearings, the maximum error amounts to about 1°.

This is acceptable for small boat navigation. You can also take an amplitude of the sun when it is rising or setting, and this will provide the sun's true bearing. All you have to know is the date and the approximate latitude. The tables included in the following chapter will enable even a novice to do this painlessly, without referring to other material.

6

✳

An Explanation
of Compass
Correction Tables

TWO SIMPLE tables are included in this text to provide the observer with the true bearing of the Sun and the North Star, Polaris.

The first of these, The Quick and Easy Compass Corrector, is a condensed table of amplitudes that gives the sun's true bearings when it is rising or setting. These are accurate to the nearest degree. The sun's bearing should be taken when its lower limb (the bottom rim) is about half of its diameter above the horizon. The tables are entered with the observer's *latitude* to the nearest degree and the *declination* indicated for the date most closely corresponding to the date of observation. The amplitude derived is then applied to the east point (90°) when the sun is rising, or the west point (270°) when the sun is setting, according to the instructions and examples shown at the bottom of the tables and in the diagram below. These demonstrate how the amplitudes are applied to obtain the true bearing.

Declination N+	Declination N-
270°	090°
Declination S-	Declination S+

Those interested in more accurate amplitudes, or amplitudes for latitudes greater than 45°, may refer to Appendix A, which contains Table 27 from Volume II of *Bowditch Publication No. 9,* or compute their own amplitude with a calculator, using the formula
SINE OF THE AMPLITUDE = SINE OF THE DECLINATION ÷ COSINE OF THE LATITUDE.

The second table, the Quick and Easy Skyclock, provides the observer with the true bearing of the star Polaris for compass correction purposes. As a fringe benefit, you can also determine your latitude by sextant observations of this same star. In order to do this, you must become familiar with two well known constellations. The most important is the Big Dipper (Ursa Major). The two stars that form the side

KMA COMPASS CORRECTOR

Calendar Tables (Declination)

DEC.	0°	1°	2°	3°	4°	5°	6°	7°	8°	9°	10°	11°	12°	13°	14°	15°	16°	17°	18°	19°	20°	21°	22°	23°
N (MAR–JUN)	Mar 21	Mar 23	Mar 26	Mar 28	Mar 31	Apr 3	Apr 5	Apr 8	Apr 11	Apr 13	Apr 16	Apr 19	Apr 22	Apr 25	Apr 28	May 1	May 5	May 8	May 12	May 16	May 21	May 26	Jun 1	Jun 10
N (SEP–JUN)	Sep 23	Sep 21	Sep 18	Sep 16	Sep 13	Sep 10	Sep 8	Sep 5	Sep 2	Aug 30	Aug 28	Aug 25	Aug 22	Aug 19	Aug 16	Aug 13	Aug 9	Aug 5	Aug 2	Jul 28	Jul 24	Jul 19	Jul 10	Jul 3
S (SEP–DEC)	Sep 23	Sep 26	Sep 28	Oct 1	Oct 3	Oct 6	Oct 9	Oct 11	Oct 14	Oct 17	Oct 19	Oct 22	Oct 25	Oct 28	Oct 31	Nov 2	Nov 5	Nov 8	Nov 14	Nov 17	Nov 21	Nov 26	Dec 3	Dec 11
S (MAR–DEC)	Mar 21	Mar 18	Mar 16	Mar 13	Mar 11	Mar 8	Mar 6	Mar 3	Mar 1	Feb 26	Feb 23	Feb 20	Feb 18	Feb 15	Feb 12	Feb 9	Feb 5	Feb 2	Jan 29	Jan 25	Jan 21	Jan 16	Jan 10	Dec 2

AMPLITUDES

LAT.	0°	1°	2°	3°	4°	5°	6°	7°	8°	9°	10°	11°	12°	13°	14°	15°	16°	17°	18°	19°	20°	21°	22°	23°
0°–11°	0°	1°	2°	3°	4°	5°	6°	7°	8°	9°	10°	11°	12°	13°	14°	15°	16°	17°	18°	19°	20°	21°	22°	23°
12°–19°	0°	1°	2°	3°	4°	5°	6°	7°	8°	9°	10°	11°	12°	13°	14°	15°	16°	17°	18°	19°	21°	22°	23°	24°
20°–24°	0°	1°	2°	3°	4°	5°	6°	7°	8°	9°	11°	12°	13°	14°	15°	16°	17°	18°	20°	21°	22°	23°	24°	25°
25°–28°	0°	1°	2°	3°	4°	6°	7°	8°	9°	10°	11°	12°	13°	15°	16°	17°	18°	19°	21°	22°	23°	24°	25°	26°
29°–32°	0°	1°	2°	3°	5°	6°	7°	8°	10°	11°	12°	13°	14°	16°	17°	18°	19°	20°	22°	23°	24°	25°	26°	27°
33°–35°	0°	1°	2°	4°	5°	6°	7°	9°	10°	11°	12°	14°	15°	16°	18°	19°	20°	21°	22°	24°	25°	26°	27°	28°
36°–37°	0°	1°	3°	4°	5°	6°	8°	9°	10°	12°	13°	14°	16°	17°	18°	20°	21°	22°	23°	25°	26°	27°	28°	29°
38°–39°	0°	1°	3°	4°	5°	7°	8°	9°	11°	12°	14°	15°	16°	18°	19°	20°	22°	23°	24°	26°	27°	28°	29°	30°
40°–41°	0°	2°	3°	4°	6°	7°	8°	10°	11°	13°	14°	15°	17°	18°	20°	21°	22°	24°	25°	27°	28°	29°	30°	31°
42°–43°	0°	2°	3°	4°	6°	7°	9°	10°	12°	13°	15°	16°	18°	19°	21°	22°	23°	25°	26°	28°	29°	30°	31°	32°
44°–45°	0°	2°	3°	5°	6°	7°	9°	10°	12°	13°	15°	16°	18°	19°	21°	22°	24°	25°	26°	28°	29°	31°	32°	33°

The true bearing of the sun may be determined when it is rising or setting, by entering the tables with the LATITUDE of the observer and the DECLINATION of the sun to the nearest degree. The Amplitude indicated is preceded by the Prefix "E" or "W" depending whether the sun is rising "E" or setting "W" and is followed by the suffix "N" or "S" in accordance with the direction of the sun's declination, for example:

Latitude of observer: 23° – Declination 15° N a.m. E 16° N = 074°
p.m. W 16° N = 286°

Latitude of observer: 23° – Declination 15° S a.m. E 16° S = 106°
p.m. W 16° S = 254°

For greatest accuracy, the sun's bearing should be observed when it is approximately 1/2 a diameter above the horizon.

The Declination may be found by entering the Calendar Tables and taking the Value over the Date which most closely corresponds to the date of observation. The upper two lines indicate N'ly Declination, the lower two lines indicate S'ly Declination.

KMA – NAVIGATION SYSTEMS   © G. H. Reid

of the dipper away from the handle are called the "pointers." A line drawn through them from the bottom of the dipper will point to the North Star. Almost opposite the dipper is a constellation called Cassiopeia. It is shaped like a wobbly W, with the top of the W pointing toward Polaris. These constellations are easily recognized once you are acquainted with them. At least one of them is visible on any clear night north of the equator.

Polaris is not a first magnitude star, and may be hard to see at latitudes south of 10° to 12° N, and of course it cannot be seen at all south of the equator.

When Polaris is visible, it will permit you to determine your compass error readily. It can also provide an easy method of determining your latitude. In the latter case, you must have a good horizon at dawn or dusk, or enough illumination from the moon to provide a good horizon so that you can take an accurate sextant altitude.

The Quick and Easy Skyclock is intended to permit you to use both of these functions without referring to other tables, or even having an accurate timepiece.

In order to use the Skyclock, the reader should refer to Sheet B with the corrections for altitude and bearing shown around the perimeter at one-hour intervals. On Sheet A the pointers of the Big Dipper are considered as the hour hand, and by estimating its position relative to Sheet B, you can determine the correction for altitude observations (upper figure) and the star's true bearing (lower figure).

Both of these sheets can be laminated, and Sheet A can be attached to Sheet B so that it rotates about the center. You then estimate the correction to both the bearing and the altitude by placing the hour hand in the same relative position as the pointers in the heavens.

Sextant observations are corrected by applying the standard corrections for stars and "dip" (height of eye) to the sextant altitude (Hs) to calculate the observed altitude (Ho). The correction noted on the Skyclock is then added or subtracted to the Ho to determine your latitude. Note the example below:

Sextant Altitude (Hs)	27°	18'.0
Star Alt. Correction		-1'.8
Height of Eye (Dip) 10'		-3'.1
Observed Altitude	27°	13'.1
Skyclock Correction (10 o'clock)		+37'.4
Latitude	27°	50'.5 N

The corrections to sextant observations of Polaris are easier to estimate when the hand is between 5 and 6 o'clock and 11 and 12 o'clock. The accuracy of sights taken when the pointers are in these positions is comparable to sights worked out by conventional methods. Sights taken at other times or where the correction must be interpolated are usually accurate within three to five miles.

QUICK AND EASY SKYCLOCK

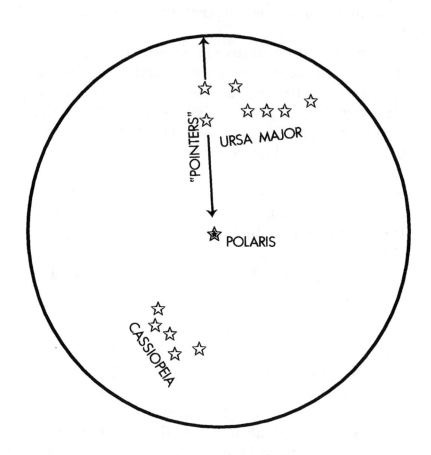

SHEET A

QUICK AND EASY SKYCLOCK

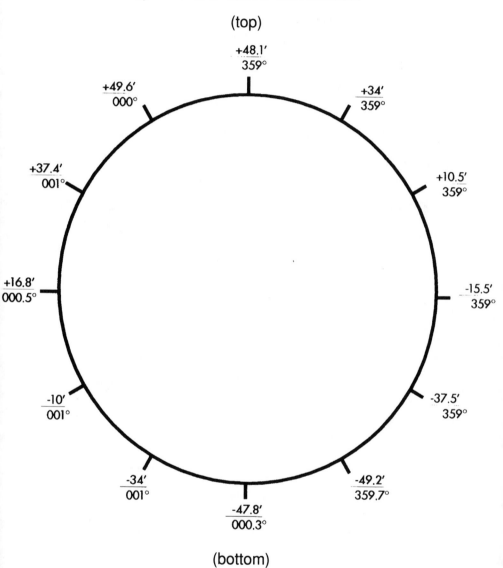

(top)

+48.1'
359°

+49.6'
000°

+34'
359°

+37.4'
001°

+10.5'
359°

+16.8'
000.5°

-15.5'
359°

-10'
001°

-37.5'
359°

-34'
001°

-49.2'
359.7°

-47.8'
000.3°

(bottom)

SHEET B

• 29 •

CORRECTIONS TO SEXTANT ALTITUDES (Hs)

SEXTANT ALTITUDE		DIP	
Hs	Correction.	Ht. of Eye	Correction
10°-00'	-5'.3	4 ft.	-1'.9
12°-00'	-4'.5	6 ft.	-2'.4
15°-00'	-3'.6	8 ft.	-2'.7
20°-00'	-2'.6	10 ft.	-3'.1
25°-00'	-2'.0	12 ft.	-3'.4
30°-00'	-1'.6	15 ft.	-3'.8
40°-00'	-1'.2	20 ft.	-4'.3
50°-00'	-0'.8	25 ft.	-4'.8

7

✳

Swinging Ship:
How to Set Up a
Deviation Table

I T HAS ALREADY been noted that a compass is
not of much use unless its error is known. We
also know that deviation is not constant on all
headings and that a vessel may be required to steer
many different courses.

In view of these facts, it is obvious that there
should be some means close at hand for you to be
able to determine, with reasonable accuracy, the

compass error on any heading you are required to steer. If the vessel has any deviation at all, there should be a current Deviation Table posted either near the helm or over the chart table for this purpose.

In order to do this, you should "swing ship." This means turning the vessel through the 360° circle of the compass, steadying up at uniform intervals 15° to 30° apart, and taking bearings at each interval to determine the compass error on each of these headings. I sometimes take a shortcut and swing the ship only through an arc of 90° or 180°, if all of my anticipated courses lie within that limited quadrant or sector of the compass.

It is best to set up a Deviation Card beforehand showing the compass heading (PSC), the compass bearing (PSC Ø) of the object, or range, and the true bearing (True Ø). By applying the *variation* to the compass error in accordance with the established rules, the *deviation* is found and shown in the right-hand column. PSC means "per standard compass," and Ø is the symbol for "bearing."

Note the examples shown on the following page.

COMPASS CORRECTION CARD

PSC HEADING	PSC Ø	TRUE Ø	COMPASS ERROR	VARIATION	DEVIATION
000°	081°	078°	3°W	3°W	0°
015°	083°	078°	5°W	3°W	2°W
030°	085°	078°	7°W	3°W	4°W
045°	081°	078°	3°W	3°W	3°W
060°	079°	078°	1°W	3°W	2°E
075°	077°	078°	1°E	3°W	4°E
090°	075°	078°	3°E	3°W	6°E
etc.					

Afterward, the observer can make a deviation table like the one shown below:

PSC HEADING	DEVIATION
000°	0°
015°	2°W
030°	4°W
045°	3°W
060°	2°E
075°	4°E
090°	6°E
etc.	

PSC (per standard compass)
PSC Ø (per standard compass bearing)
True Ø (true bearing)

8

Adjusting the Compass

MOST SMALL boats do not need the compass adjusted unless they are built of steel. This doesn't mean that there is no deviation. There might be, but the usual cause is due to the proximity of electrical or electronic equipment. In this case, it is better to move this gear to a new location away from the compass, or vice versa, so that the compass will not be affected.

Ordinarily, I do not adjust boat compasses unless the deviation exceeds 7° or 8°. Compasses tend to oscillate a bit if the boat is rolling, and interpolating for courses that fall between the headings on the Deviation Card is uncertain. However, if it is necessary to adjust the compass, the methods used are simple enough for anyone to master. But there are a few things that you must do beforehand.

1. Remove any bubbles from the compass. This is done by rotating the compass so that the bubble is under the filling plug. A 50/50 mixture of *grain* alcohol and water, or kerosene (if an oil-base liquid is used) is injected into the compass with a syringe. The two substances are not compatible. Hundred-proof Vodka works fine for alcohol filled compasses, and you can toast your handiwork with the leftovers. *Do not* use wood alcohol for this purpose, as it becomes cloudy and might discolor the compass card.

2. If the compass has two metal spheres (quadrantal correctors) mounted on either side, these should be moved as close to the compass as possible and rotated. If this deflects the compass more than 2°, they should be removed and annealed (heated to a dull red and allowed to cool slowly). The position of these spheres when the adjustment is started should be as far outboard as possible.

3. Determine what you will use for bearings. If you are at sea, remember that it will require about an hour to adjust the compass. If you are in the

northern hemisphere, you can use Polaris. But if you can't use Polaris, and don't know how to work out an azimuth, refer to the sun's bearing at the bottom of the page in *Publication 260* that corresponds to your latitude and declination and note the changes of this bearing at 10-minute intervals that follow daybreak.

4. Have your tools at hand. You'll need a screwdriver, compensating magnets, brass fittings and screws, a pelorus (if needed), and some duct seal, putty, other mastic compound, or tape to hold the magnets temporarily in place while you swing ship.

5. Some compasses have internal magnets that are affixed within the binnacle. They are usually marked E-W and N-S and can be adjusted with a screwdriver.

6. If the compass is frozen, the initial adjustment should be made on a heading different from the one that the compass is attracted to so that the effect is apparent.

THE ADJUSTMENTS

The fore-and-aft magnets, usually located alongside the compass in boats, are called the B magnets and are used to adjust the deviation of the east-west headings

(090° - 270°). The athwartship magnets are usually located forward of the compass and are called the C magnets. They are used to compensate for deviation on the north-south headings (000° - 180°).

1. Come to a cardinal magnetic heading, e.g., *east* (090°). Place the fore-and-aft B magnets in such a manner that all deviation is removed.

2. Come to a *south* magnetic heading (180°). Place athwartship C magnets to remove all deviation.

3. Come to a *west* magnetic heading (270°). Correct half of any observed deviation by moving the B magnet.

4. Come to a *north* magnetic heading (000°). Correct half of any observed deviation by moving the C magnets.

5. Come to any intercardinal heading, e.g., *northeast* (045°). Correct any observed deviation by moving the spheres in or out.

6. Come to the next intercardinal heading, e.g., *southeast* (135°). Correct half of any observed deviation by moving the spheres.

7. Secure all correctors before swinging for residual deviation, and list the deviations on the Deviation Table.

The reader should refer to the table below for a simplified explanation of the mechanics involved.

THE PLACEMENT OF THE FORE-AND-AFT AND ATHWARTSHIP MAGNETS

DEVIATION MAGNETS → ↓	Easterly on east Westerly on west (+ B error)	Westerly on east Easterly on west (– B error)
No fore-and-aft magnets	Place magnets right of compass, red end forward.	Place magnets right of compass, red end aft.
Fore-and-aft magnets. Red end forward (right of compass)	Move magnets toward compass	Move magnets away from compass
Fore-and-aft magnets, red end aft (right of compass).	Move magnets away from compass	Move magnets toward compass
DEVIATION MAGNETS → ↓	Easterly on north Westerly on south (+ C error)	Westerly on north Easterly on south (– C error)
No athwartship magnet.	Place athwartship magnet forward of compass, red starboard	Place athwartship magnet forward of compass, red port
Athwartship magnet, red starboard.	Move magnet closer to compass	Move magnet away from compass
Athwartship magnet, red port.	Move magnet away from compass	Move magnet closer to compass

9

✳

Summary

THE INFORMATION and tables contained in this text are intended for both pleasure and commercial boaters. They detail the methods and means for determining compass error, and correcting or compensating it. The Skyclock also provides a simple way to calculate latitude by sextant observations of Polaris.

If the methods seem a bit "rough cut," this is deliberate. References to flinders bars, heeling magnets, degaussing systems, and much theory have been dispensed with in the interest of brevity. The text was written this way because not many small vessels have flinders bars, heeling magnets, or degaussing systems aboard. The small vessels referred to also include many offshore draggers, ocean-going tugs, "oil patch" supply boats, as well as pleasure craft.

The Compass Corrector tables have been rounded off to the nearest degree for convenience. One can take bearings and plot courses that are accurate to a half-degree on a loaded supertanker (a very stable platform), but this is seldom done. It is unlikely that it would be possible to come closer than a degree on a small vessel rolling in a seaway, with a compass card only three or four inches in diameter.

In a voyage of a thousand miles, an error of 1° in the course amounts to about 17.5 miles. This could be critical if the seagoer fails to anticipate this possibility and neglects to determine his position at intermediate positions. In this case, he would be either unrealistic or foolish - after all, certain allowances have to be made for errors in steering and corrected as needed.

I have no quarrel with those who pursue greater accuracy. A list of sources of information for this purpose is included for those who wish to pursue this goal. However, one should bear in mind that there are few absolutes at sea, and most seafarers fare better if they salt the science of navigation with the seasoning of art.

Some useful publications with information applicable to the subjects addressed in this text are published by the Defense Mapping Agency Hydrographic/Topographic Center (DMAHTC). They are listed below:

Publication 260: "Red" *Azimuth Tables*
Publication 9: Bowditch, Volumes I & II, Tables 27 - 28
Publication 226: Handbook of Magnetic Compass Adjustment
Publication 249: Volumes I, II and III
Publication 229 for observer's azimuth
The *Nautical Almanac,* published by the U.S. Government Printing Office.

These can be obtained from the chart agents listed on pages 46-47 or directly from

NOAA Distribution Branch (N/CG33)
National Ocean Service
Riverdale, MD 20737-1199
Tel. (301) 436-6990 or 1-800-638-8972 or
    1-800-638-8975
Fax (301) 436-6829

In the U.K., the *Nautical Almanac* is published by HMSO. The *Sight Reduction Tables,* No. AP 3270, in three volumes (HMSO) are the equivalent to *Publication 249.*

10

Sources of Nautical Books, Charts and Navigational Instruments

INFORMATION and equipment for the navigator or sailor interested in compass correction and other related subjects may not be readily available. For those whose sources are limited in this respect, the companies listed below provide convenient and comprehensive outlets where these supplies can be ordered.

CHARTS AND PUBLICATIONS

Armchair Sailor Bookstore
543 Thames St.
Newport, RI 02840
Tel. (401) 847-4252
Fax (401) 847-1219

Baker Lyman and Co., Inc. Charts
3220 South 1-10 Service Road
Metairie, LA 70001
Tel. (504) 535-3685
Fax (504) 831-3786
Toll Free: 1-800-535-6956

Baker Lyman and Co., Inc.
8876 Gulf Freeway S., Suite 110
Houston, TX 77017
Tel. (713) 943-7032
Fax (713) 943-3096
Toll Free: 1-800-527-3154

Bluewater Books & Charts
1481 SE 17th Street Causeway
Ft. Lauderdale, FL 33316
Tel. (954) 763-6533
Fax (954) 522-2278

INSTRUMENTS AND PUBLICATIONS

Celestaire, Inc.
416 S. Pershing
Wichita, KS 67218
Tel. (316) 686-9785
Fax (316) 686-8926

Note that both Baker Lyman and Bluewater Books & Charts have an extensive inventory of books, charts, and the tools of the trade. The publications are listed in their catalogues.

Celestaire's catalogue carries a wide list of nautical instruments, including calculators, peloruses, sextants, short-wave radios, etc. They also publish a Nautical Almanac with the same information as that provided by the government edition, but at a substantially lower price.

RECOMMENDED SOURCES IN THE U.K.

Kelvin Hughes
142 The Minories
London EC3N 1NH
Tel. 0171 709 9076
Fax 0171 481 1298

Captain O.M. Watts
7 Dover Street
London WIX 3PJ
Tel. 0171 493 4633
Fax 0171 495 0755

Appendices

The two appendices that follow are drawn respectively from Volumes I and II of *Bowditch Publication No. 9.* The first appendix is a Long-Term Almanac that will provide the reader with a more concise declination for observations of the sun's bearing when rising or setting.

The second appendix includes Table 27 from Volume II of *Publication No. 9.* It will provide the observer with amplitudes of the sun at latitudes as high as 77°. A table of declinations is on the opposite page.

APPENDIX ONE

This table is used to determine the declination of the sun. It is based upon the fact that approximately correct values for Greenwich Hour Angle (GHA) and declination of the sun can be obtained from an Almanac that is exactly four years out of date. 0 represents leap year (i.e., a year evenly divisible by the number 4). The observer should count the number of years the present year is from the last leap year and select the appropriate year for the declination and GHA.

The GHA - 175° and declination of the sun are given at intervals of three days throughout the four-year cycle, except the final days of each month, when the interval varies between one and four days. Linear interpolation is made between entries to obtain data for a given day. Additional corrections to the GHA of the sun of 15° per hour, 15' per minute, and 15" per second are made to obtain the GHA at a given time. Declination of the sun is obtained to sufficient accuracy by linear interpolation alone.

SUN

0 GHA −175°	0 Dec.	Quad. GHA Corr.	1 GHA −175°	1 Dec.	Date	2 GHA −175°	2 Dec.	Quad. Dec. Corr.	3 GHA −175°	3 Dec.
JANUARY										
4 14.4	23 05.5 S	−0.11	4 09.0	23 02.0 S	1	4 10.8	23 03.1 S	−0.32	4 12.9	23 04.2 S
3 53.3	22 50.2 S	−0.13	3 48.0	22 45.6 S	4	3 49.8	22 47.0 S	−0.35	3 51.9	22 48.4 S
3 33.0	22 30.7 S	−0.12	3 27.8	22 25.1 S	7	3 29.8	22 26.8 S	−0.39	3 31.7	22 28.6 S
3 13.8	22 07.2 S	−0.09	3 08.8	22 00.6 S	10	3 10.8	22 02.7 S	−0.42	3 12.5	22 04.8 S
2 55.7	21 39.9 S	0.04	2 51.1	21 32.2 S	13	2 53.0	21 34.7 S	−0.44	2 54.5	21 37.1 S
2 38.9	21 08.7 S	+0.03	2 34.8	21 00.2 S	16	2 36.6	21 02.9 S	−0.46	2 37.9	21 05.6 S
2 23.7	20 33.9 S	+0.09	2 20.1	20 24.5 S	19	2 21.7	20 27.5 S	−0.48	2 22.9	20 30.5 S
2 10.1	19 55.6 S	+0.13	2 07.0	19 45.4 S	22	2 08.4	19 48.7 S	−0.49	2 09.5	19 51.9 S
1 58.2	19 13.9 S	+0.15	1 55.7	19 02.9 S	25	1 56.8	19 06.4 S	−0.52	1 57.9	19 10.0 S
1 48.2	18 29.1 S	+0.15	1 46.1	18 17.3 S	28	1 47.0	18 21.1 S	−0.54	1 48.0	18 24.9 S
FEBRUARY										
1 37.7	17 24.7 S	+0.13	1 36.1	17 11.9 S	1	1 36.8	17 16.0 S	−0.57	1 37.8	17 20.2 S
1 32.0	16 33.2 S	+0.14	1 30.7	16 19.6 S	4	1 31.3	16 24.0 S	−0.59	1 32.1	16 28.4 S
1 28.0	15 39.0 S	+0.15	1 27.1	15 24.8 S	7	1 27.8	15 29.5 S	−0.60	1 28.3	15 34.0 S
1 25.9	14 42.5 S	+0.19	1 25.4	14 27.7 S	10	1 26.0	14 32.5 S	−0.61	1 26.3	14 37.2 S
1 25.4	13 43.6 S	+0.24	1 25.4	13 28.4 S	13	1 25.9	13 33.4 S	−0.60	1 26.0	13 38.2 S
1 26.7	12 42.8 S	+0.29	1 27.2	12 27.1 S	16	1 27.5	12 32.3 S	−0.60	1 27.4	12 37.2 S
1 29.6	11 40.1 S	+0.34	1 30.6	11 24.0 S	19	1 30.7	11 29.3 S	−0.59	1 30.4	11 34.4 S
1 34.0	10 35.8 S	+0.36	1 35.6	10 19.3 S	22	1 35.4	10 24.7 S	−0.59	1 35.1	10 30.0 S
1 40.0	9 30.0 S	+0.36	1 41.9	9 13.2 S	25	1 41.5	9 18.6 S	−0.60	1 41.2	9 24.1 S
1 47.4	8 23.0 S	+0.34	1 49.5	8 05.8 S	28	1 49.0	8 11.3 S	−0.61	1 48.7	8 17.0 S
MARCH										
1 52.9	7 37.6 S	+0.32	1 52.3	7 43.1 S	1	1 51.7	7 48.7 S	−0.62	1 51.4	7 54.3 S
2 02.3	6 28.8 S	+0.31	2 01.4	6 34.4 S	4	2 00.8	6 40.0 S	−0.62	2 00.4	6 45.7 S
2 12.6	5 19.2 S	+0.31	2 11.6	5 24.8 S	7	2 11.0	5 30.5 S	−0.62	2 10.5	5 36.3 S
2 23.8	4 08.9 S	+0.33	2 22.6	4 14.5 S	10	2 22.1	4 20.4 S	−0.61	2 21.4	4 26.1 S
2 35.7	2 58.2 S	+0.36	2 34.5	3 03.8 S	13	2 33.9	3 09.7 S	−0.59	2 33.1	3 15.5 S
2 48.2	1 47.1 S	+0.40	2 47.1	1 52.8 S	16	2 46.4	1 58.7 S	−0.56	2 45.4	2 04.5 S
3 01.1	0 35.9 S	+0.43	3 00.1	0 41.7 S	19	2 59.4	0 47.6 S	−0.54	2 58.3	0 53.3 S
3 14.5	0 35.2 N	+0.44	3 13.6	0 29.4 N	22	3 12.7	0 23.6 N	+0.53	3 11.6	0 17.8 N
3 28.1	1 46.1 N	+0.43	3 27.2	1 40.3 N	25	3 26.2	1 34.6 N	+0.52	3 25.2	1 28.8 N
3 41.9	2 56.6 N	+0.40	3 40.9	2 50.9 N	28	3 39.8	2 45.2 N	+0.52	3 38.9	2 39.4 N
APRIL										
4 00.0	4 29.8 N	+0.35	3 59.0	4 24.3 N	1	3 57.9	4 18.6 N	+0.52	3 57.1	4 12.8 N
4 13.4	5 38.9 N	+0.33	4 12.3	5 33.4 N	4	4 11.2	5 27.8 N	+0.51	4 10.5	5 22.1 N
4 26.4	6 47.1 N	+0.32	4 25.2	6 41.7 N	7	4 24.3	6 36.2 N	+0.49	4 23.5	6 30.6 N
4 38.8	7 54.3 N	+0.33	4 37.7	7 49.0 N	10	4 36.9	7 43.5 N	+0.47	4 36.0	7 38.0 N
4 50.6	9 00.3 N	+0.35	4 49.6	8 55.1 N	13	4 48.9	8 49.7 N	+0.44	4 48.0	8 44.3 N
5 01.7	10 05.0 N	+0.37	5 00.9	9 59.8 N	16	5 00.2	9 54.5 N	+0.41	4 59.2	9 49.3 N
5 12.0	11 08.1 N	+0.39	5 11.3	11 03.0 N	19	5 10.6	10 57.9 N	+0.39	5 09.7	10 52.8 N
5 21.4	12 09.6 N	+0.37	5 20.9	12 04.6 N	22	5 20.0	11 59.7 N	+0.37	5 19.3	11 54.7 N
5 29.8	13 09.2 N	+0.33	5 29.4	13 04.4 N	25	5 28.5	12 59.7 N	+0.36	5 28.0	12 54.8 N
5 37.2	14 06.9 N	+0.28	5 36.8	14 02.3 N	28	5 36.0	13 57.7 N	+0.34	5 35.6	13 53.0 N
MAY										
5 43.4	15 02.6 N	+0.24	5 43.0	14 58.1 N	1	5 42.3	14 53.7 N	+0.33	5 42.1	14 49.2 N
5 48.4	15 56.0 N	+0.20	5 48.0	15 51.7 N	4	5 47.5	15 47.5 N	+0.31	5 47.3	15 43.1 N
5 52.1	16 47.0 N	+0.19	5 51.7	16 43.0 N	7	5 51.4	16 38.9 N	+0.28	5 51.3	16 34.7 N
5 54.5	17 35.5 N	+0.19	5 54.2	17 31.7 N	10	5 54.1	17 27.8 N	+0.25	5 53.9	17 23.9 N
5 55.6	18 21.4 N	+0.21	5 55.5	18 17.7 N	13	5 55.5	18 14.1 N	+0.22	5 55.3	18 10.4 N
5 55.4	19 04.5 N	+0.23	5 55.5	19 01.0 N	16	5 55.5	18 57.6 N	+0.19	5 55.4	18 54.2 N
5 53.9	19 44.7 N	+0.23	5 54.3	19 41.4 N	19	5 54.3	19 38.3 N	+0.16	5 54.3	19 35.1 N
5 51.3	20 21.8 N	+0.20	5 51.8	20 18.8 N	22	5 51.7	20 15.9 N	+0.13	5 51.9	20 13.0 N
5 47.5	20 55.8 N	+0.16	5 48.1	20 53.1 N	25	5 48.0	20 50.5 N	+0.11	5 48.4	20 47.7 N
5 42.6	21 26.6 N	+0.11	5 43.2	21 24.2 N	28	5 43.2	21 21.8 N	+0.08	5 43.8	21 19.3 N
JUNE										
5 34.5	22 02.4 N	+0.04	5 35.1	22 00.4 N	1	5 35.2	21 58.3 N	+0.04	5 36.0	21 56.2 N
5 27.4	22 25.3 N	+0.02	5 27.9	22 23.5 N	4	5 28.2	22 21.7 N	+0.01	5 28.9	22 19.9 N
5 19.4	22 44.6 N	+0.02	5 19.9	22 43.1 N	7	5 20.4	22 41.6 N	−0.02	5 21.1	22 40.1 N
5 10.7	23 00.3 N	+0.04	5 11.3	22 59.1 N	10	5 11.9	22 57.9 N	−0.05	5 12.5	22 56.7 N
5 01.5	23 12.4 N	+0.07	5 02.3	23 11.5 N	13	5 02.9	23 10.6 N	−0.08	5 03.4	23 09.7 N
4 51.9	23 20.8 N	+0.09	4 52.8	23 20.2 N	16	4 53.4	23 19.6 N	−0.12	4 53.9	23 19.0 N
4 42.1	23 25.5 N	+0.08	4 43.2	23 25.3 N	19	4 43.6	23 24.9 N	−0.15	4 44.2	23 24.6 N
4 32.4	23 26.5 N	+0.06	4 33.4	23 26.6 N	22	4 33.7	23 26.5 N	−0.18	4 34.5	23 26.5 N
4 22.8	23 23.8 N	+0.01	4 23.8	23 24.1 N	25	4 24.0	23 24.4 N	−0.22	4 24.8	23 24.6 N
4 13.4	23 17.4 N	−0.03	4 14.3	23 18.0 N	28	4 14.5	23 18.5 N	−0.25	4 15.4	23 19.1 N

SUN

GHA −175°	0 Dec.	Quad. GHA Corr.	GHA −175°	1 Dec.	Date	GHA −175°	2 Dec.	Quad. Dec. Corr.	GHA −175°	3 Dec.
					JULY					
4 04.5	23 07.3 N	− 0.06	4 05.2	23 08.2 N	1	4 05.4	23 09.0 N	− 0.28	4 06.3	23 09.9 N
3 56.1	22 53.5 N	− 0.07	3 56.6	22 54.7 N	4	3 57.0	22 55.8 N	− 0.31	3 57.7	22 57.0 N
3 48.4	22 36.2 N	− 0.05	3 48.8	22 37.6 N	7	3 49.2	22 39.1 N	− 0.34	3 49.8	22 40.5 N
3 41.5	22 15.3 N	− 0.01	3 41.9	22 17.1 N	10	3 42.3	22 18.8 N	− 0.37	3 42.7	22 20.5 N
3 35.5	21 51.0 N	+ 0.03	3 36.0	21 53.0 N	13	3 36.2	21 55.0 N	− 0.39	3 36.4	21 57.0 N
3 30.6	21 23.3 N	+ 0.05	3 31.1	21 25.7 N	16	3 31.1	21 27.9 N	− 0.41	3 31.3	21 30.1 N
3 26.9	20 52.4 N	+ 0.06	3 27.4	20 55.0 N	19	3 27.2	20 57.5 N	− 0.44	3 27.4	21 00.0 N
3 24.5	20 18.3 N	+ 0.04	3 24.9	20 21.2 N	22	3 24.5	20 23.8 N	− 0.47	3 24.7	20 26.6 N
3 23.4	19 41.1 N	+ 0.01	3 23.6	19 44.2 N	25	3 23.0	19 47.1 N	− 0.50	3 23.3	19 50.2 N
3 23.6	19 01.0 N	− 0.02	3 23.6	19 04.3 N	28	3 23.0	19 07.5 N	− 0.54	3 23.1	19 10.8 N
					AUGUST					
3 26.0	18 03.2 N	− 0.03	3 25.6	18 06.8 N	1	3 25.1	18 10.3 N	− 0.57	3 25.1	18 13.9 N
3 29.3	17 16.7 N	− 0.02	3 28.8	17 20.5 N	4	3 28.2	17 24.2 N	− 0.59	3 28.0	17 28.0 N
3 33.9	16 27.7 N	+ 0.02	3 33.4	16 31.6 N	7	3 32.8	16 35.6 N	− 0.60	3 32.3	16 39.6 N
3 39.9	15 36.3 N	+ 0.06	3 39.3	15 40.4 N	10	3 38.6	15 44.6 N	− 0.60	3 38.0	15 48.7 N
3 47.1	14 42.6 N	+ 0.09	3 46.5	14 47.0 N	13	3 45.7	14 51.3 N	− 0.61	3 44.9	14 55.6 N
3 55.7	13 46.8 N	+ 0.11	3 55.0	13 51.4 N	16	3 54.0	13 55.8 N	− 0.62	3 53.2	14 00.3 N
4 05.4	12 49.1 N	+ 0.11	4 04.7	12 53.9 N	19	4 03.4	12 58.4 N	− 0.64	4 02.7	13 03.1 N
4 16.2	11 49.6 N	+ 0.09	4 15.4	11 54.5 N	22	4 14.0	11 59.1 N	− 0.66	4 13.3	12 04.0 N
4 28.1	10 48.4 N	+ 0.06	4 27.2	10 53.3 N	25	4 25.7	10 58.1 N	− 0.68	4 24.9	11 03.2 N
4 40.9	9 45.6 N	+ 0.03	4 39.8	9 50.6 N	28	4 38.3	9 55.6 N	− 0.70	4 37.5	10 00.8 N
					SEPTEMBER					
4 59.2	8 19.8 N	+ 0.02	4 57.9	8 24.9 N	1	4 56.5	8 30.0 N	− 0.71	4 55.6	8 35.4 N
5 13.7	7 13.9 N	+ 0.04	5 12.3	7 19.2 N	4	5 10.9	7 24.4 N	− 0.70	5 09.9	7 29.8 N
5 28.7	6 07.0 N	+ 0.08	5 27.3	6 12.4 N	7	5 26.0	6 17.8 N	− 0.69	5 24.7	6 23.2 N
5 44.1	4 59.2 N	+ 0.11	5 42.8	5 04.7 N	10	5 41.4	5 10.1 N	− 0.68	5 40.1	5 15.6 N
5 59.9	3 50.7 N	+ 0.13	5 58.6	3 56.2 N	13	5 57.1	4 01.7 N	− 0.67	5 55.8	4 07.2 N
6 15.8	2 41.5 N	+ 0.13	6 14.7	2 47.1 N	16	6 13.0	2 52.6 N	− 0.67	6 11.7	2 58.2 N
6 31.9	1 31.9 N	+ 0.11	6 30.7	1 37.5 N	19	6 29.0	1 43.0 N	− 0.68	6 27.8	1 48.7 N
6 47.9	0 21.9 N	+ 0.08	6 46.6	0 27.6 N	22	6 44.9	0 33.1 N	− 0.68	6 43.8	0 38.8 N
7 03.6	0 48.1 S	+ 0.04	7 02.3	0 42.5 S	25	7 00.6	0 37.0 S	+ 0.69	6 59.6	0 31.2 S
7 19.0	1 58.3 S	+ 0.01	7 17.6	1 52.7 S	28	7 16.1	1 47.1 S	+ 0.68	7 15.1	1 41.3 S
					OCTOBER					
7 33.8	3 08.2 S	0.00	7 32.4	3 02.7 S	1	7 31.0	2 57.1 S	+ 0.67	7 30.0	2 51.4 S
7 48.0	4 17.9 S	+ 0.02	7 46.6	4 12.4 S	4	7 45.4	4 06.8 S	+ 0.65	7 44.3	4 01.2 S
8 01.3	5 27.2 S	+ 0.05	8 00.1	5 21.7 S	7	7 59.0	5 16.1 S	+ 0.62	7 57.9	5 10.5 S
8 13.7	6 35.8 S	+ 0.07	8 12.7	6 30.3 S	10	8 11.6	6 24.8 S	+ 0.60	8 10.5	6 19.3 S
8 25.1	7 43.6 S	+ 0.08	8 24.3	7 38.1 S	13	8 23.2	7 32.8 S	+ 0.57	8 22.2	7 27.3 S
8 35.4	8 50.5 S	+ 0.07	8 34.7	8 45.0 S	16	8 33.6	8 39.8 S	+ 0.56	8 32.8	8 34.4 S
8 44.4	9 56.2 S	+ 0.04	8 43.8	9 50.9 S	19	8 42.8	9 45.7 S	+ 0.54	8 42.2	9 40.3 S
8 52.0	11 00.6 S	− 0.01	8 51.5	10 55.4 S	22	8 50.5	10 50.3 S	+ 0.53	8 50.1	10 45.0 S
8 58.1	12 03.5 S	− 0.05	8 57.6	11 58.5 S	25	8 56.9	11 53.5 S	+ 0.52	8 56.6	11 48.3 S
9 02.6	13 04.7 S	− 0.08	9 02.1	12 59.9 S	28	9 01.6	12 55.0 S	+ 0.50	9 01.5	12 50.0 S
					NOVEMBER					
9 05.8	14 23.5 S	− 0.09	9 05.5	14 18.9 S	1	9 05.4	14 14.2 S	+ 0.46	9 05.3	14 09.4 S
9 06.1	15 20.3 S	− 0.07	9 06.0	15 15.8 S	4	9 06.1	15 11.2 S	+ 0.42	9 06.0	15 06.6 S
9 04.6	16 14.7 S	− 0.04	9 04.7	16 10.4 S	7	9 05.0	16 06.0 S	+ 0.38	9 04.9	16 01.6 S
9 01.1	17 06.7 S	− 0.03	9 01.6	17 02.5 S	10	9 01.9	16 58.4 S	+ 0.35	9 02.0	16 54.2 S
8 55.8	17 56.1 S	− 0.03	8 56.5	17 52.1 S	13	8 56.9	17 48.2 S	+ 0.31	8 57.2	17 44.2 S
8 48.6	18 42.6 S	− 0.05	8 49.5	18 38.8 S	16	8 49.9	18 35.2 S	+ 0.28	8 50.5	18 31.4 S
8 39.6	19 26.1 S	− 0.09	8 40.6	19 22.7 S	19	8 41.1	19 19.2 S	+ 0.25	8 41.9	19 15.7 S
8 28.7	20 06.5 S	− 0.14	8 29.8	20 03.3 S	22	8 30.5	20 00.1 S	+ 0.22	8 31.5	19 56.9 S
8 16.1	20 43.6 S	− 0.18	8 17.2	20 40.7 S	25	8 18.1	20 37.8 S	+ 0.19	8 19.3	20 34.8 S
8 01.7	21 17.2 S	− 0.20	8 02.8	21 14.6 S	28	8 04.1	21 11.9 S	+ 0.16	8 05.3	21 09.3 S
					DECEMBER					
7 45.6	21 47.3 S	− 0.18	7 46.9	21 44.9 S	1	7 48.4	21 42.5 S	+ 0.12	7 49.6	21 40.1 S
7 28.1	22 13.5 S	− 0.15	7 29.6	22 11.5 S	4	7 31.3	22 09.4 S	+ 0.08	7 32.5	22 07.3 S
7 09.3	22 35.9 S	− 0.11	7 11.0	22 34.2 S	7	7 12.8	22 32.4 S	+ 0.04	7 13.9	22 30.6 S
6 49.3	22 54.3 S	− 0.09	6 51.3	22 52.9 S	10	6 53.0	22 51.4 S	0.00	6 54.3	22 50.0 S
6 28.5	23 08.6 S	− 0.08	6 30.6	23 07.6 S	13	6 32.3	23 06.4 S	− 0.04	6 33.7	23 05.3 S
6 06.9	23 18.8 S	− 0.09	6 09.1	23 18.1 S	16	6 10.8	23 17.3 S	− 0.08	6 12.4	23 16.5 S
5 44.9	23 24.8 S	− 0.12	5 47.1	23 24.4 S	19	5 48.8	23 24.0 S	− 0.12	5 50.5	23 23.6 S
5 22.6	23 26.6 S	− 0.15	5 24.7	23 26.6 S	22	5 26.5	23 26.5 S	− 0.16	5 28.3	23 26.4 S
5 00.2	23 24.1 S	− 0.17	5 02.2	23 24.4 S	25	5 04.1	23 24.7 S	− 0.19	5 05.9	23 25.0 S
4 38.0	23 17.5 S	− 0.17	4 39.9	23 18.1 S	28	4 41.9	23 18.7 S	− 0.23	4 43.6	23 19.3 S

APPENDIX TWO

Table 27 is a complete table of amplitudes for latitudes from 0° to 77°. A table of declinations is reproduced on the opposite page for the observer's convenience. The reader may also refer to the Long-Term Almanac for finer determinations of declination.

KMA COMPASS CORRECTOR

DEC.	0°	1°	2°	3°	4°	5°	6°	7°	8°	9°	10°	11°	12°	13°	14°	15°	16°	17°	18°	19°	20°	21°	22°	23°
N	MARCH									APRIL						MAY							JUNE	
	21	23	26	28	31	3	5	8	11	13	16	19	22	25	28	1	5	8	12	16	21	26	1	10
	SEPTEMBER													AUGUST						JULY				
	23	21	18	16	13	10	8	5	2	30	28	25	22	19	16	12	9	5	2	28	24	19	12	3
S	SEPTEMBER			OCTOBER												NOVEMBER							DEC	
	23	26°	28	1	4	6	9	11	14	17	19	22	25	28	31	3	6	10	14	17	22	27	3	11
	MARCH									FEBRUARY									JANUARY					
	21	18	16	13	11	8	6	3	1	26	23	20	18	15	12	9	5	2	29	25	21	16	10	2

APPENDIX II   TABLE 27

Amplitudes

Latitude	Declination													Latitude
	0°0	0°5	1°0	1°5	2°0	2°5	3°0	3°5	4°0	4°5	5°0	5°5	6°0	
°	°	°	°	°	°	°	°	°	°	°	°	°	°	°
0	0.0	0.5	1.0	1.5	2.0	2.5	3.0	3.5	4.0	4.5	5.0	5.5	6.0	0
10	0.0	0.5	1.0	1.5	2.0	2.5	3.0	3.6	4.1	4.6	5.1	5.6	6.1	10
15	0.0	0.5	1.0	1.6	2.1	2.6	3.1	3.6	4.1	4.7	5.2	5.7	6.2	15
20	0.0	0.5	1.1	1.6	2.1	2.7	3.2	3.7	4.3	4.8	5.3	5.9	6.4	20
25	0.0	0.6	1.1	1.7	2.2	2.8	3.3	3.9	4.4	5.0	5.5	6.1	6.6	25
30	0.0	0.6	1.2	1.7	2.3	2.9	3.5	4.0	4.6	5.2	5.8	6.4	6.9	30
32	0.0	0.6	1.2	1.8	2.4	2.9	3.5	4.1	4.7	5.3	5.9	6.5	7.1	32
34	0.0	0.6	1.2	1.8	2.4	3.0	3.6	4.2	4.8	5.4	6.0	6.6	7.2	34
36	0.0	0.6	1.2	1.9	2.5	3.1	3.7	4.3	4.9	5.6	6.2	6.8	7.4	36
38	0.0	0.6	1.3	1.9	2.5	3.2	3.8	4.4	5.1	5.7	6.4	7.0	7.6	38
40	0.0	0.7	1.3	2.0	2.6	3.3	3.9	4.6	5.2	5.9	6.5	7.2	7.8	40
42	0.0	0.7	1.3	2.0	2.7	3.4	4.0	4.7	5.4	6.1	6.7	7.4	8.1	42
44	0.0	0.7	1.4	2.1	2.8	3.5	4.2	4.9	5.6	6.3	7.0	7.7	8.4	44
46	0.0	0.7	1.4	2.2	2.9	3.6	4.3	5.0	5.8	6.5	7.2	7.9	8.7	46
48	0.0	0.7	1.5	2.2	3.0	3.7	4.5	5.2	6.0	6.7	7.5	8.2	9.0	48
50	0.0	0.8	1.6	2.3	3.1	3.9	4.7	5.4	6.2	7.0	7.8	8.6	9.4	50
51	0.0	0.8	1.6	2.4	3.2	4.0	4.8	5.6	6.4	7.2	8.0	8.8	9.6	51
52	0.0	0.8	1.6	2.4	3.2	4.1	4.9	5.7	6.5	7.3	8.1	9.0	9.8	52
53	0.0	0.8	1.7	2.5	3.3	4.2	5.0	5.8	6.7	7.5	8.3	9.2	10.0	53
54	0.0	0.9	1.7	2.6	3.4	4.3	5.1	6.0	6.8	7.7	8.5	9.4	10.2	54
55	0.0	0.9	1.7	2.6	3.5	4.4	5.2	6.1	7.0	7.9	8.7	9.6	10.5	55
56	0.0	0.9	1.8	2.7	3.6	4.5	5.4	6.3	7.2	8.1	9.0	9.9	10.8	56
57	0.0	0.9	1.8	2.8	3.7	4.6	5.5	6.4	7.4	8.3	9.2	10.1	11.1	57
58	0.0	0.9	1.9	2.8	3.8	4.7	5.7	6.6	7.6	8.5	9.5	10.4	11.4	58
59	0.0	1.0	1.9	2.9	3.9	4.9	5.8	6.8	7.8	8.8	9.7	10.7	11.7	59
60	0.0	1.0	2.0	3.0	4.0	5.0	6.0	7.0	8.0	9.0	10.0	11.1	12.1	60
61	0.0	1.0	2.1	3.1	4.1	5.2	6.2	7.2	8.3	9.3	10.3	11.4	12.5	61
62	0.0	1.1	2.1	3.2	4.3	5.3	6.4	7.5	8.5	9.6	10.7	11.8	12.9	62
63	0.0	1.1	2.2	3.3	4.4	5.5	6.6	7.7	8.8	10.0	11.1	12.2	13.3	63
64	0.0	1.1	2.3	3.4	4.6	5.7	6.9	8.0	9.2	10.3	11.5	12.6	13.8	64
65.0	0.0	1.2	2.4	3.6	4.7	5.9	7.1	8.3	9.5	10.7	11.9	13.1	14.3	65.0
65.5	0.0	1.2	2.4	3.6	4.8	6.0	7.3	8.5	9.7	10.9	12.1	13.4	14.6	65.5
66.0	0.0	1.2	2.5	3.7	4.9	6.2	7.4	8.6	9.9	11.1	12.4	13.6	14.9	66.0
66.5	0.0	1.3	2.5	3.8	5.0	6.3	7.5	8.8	10.1	11.3	12.6	13.9	15.2	66.5
67.0	0.0	1.3	2.6	3.8	5.1	6.4	7.7	9.0	10.3	11.6	12.9	14.2	15.5	67.0
67.5	0.0	1.3	2.6	3.9	5.2	6.5	7.9	9.2	10.5	11.8	13.2	14.5	15.9	67.5
68.0	0.0	1.3	2.7	4.0	5.3	6.7	8.0	9.4	10.7	12.1	13.5	14.8	16.2	68.0
68.5	0.0	1.4	2.7	4.1	5.5	6.8	8.2	9.6	11.0	12.4	13.8	15.2	16.6	68.5
69.0	0.0	1.4	2.8	4.2	5.6	7.0	8.4	9.8	11.2	12.6	14.1	15.5	17.0	69.0
69.5	0.0	1.4	2.9	4.3	5.7	7.2	8.6	10.0	11.5	12.9	14.4	15.9	17.4	69.5
70.0	0.0	1.5	2.9	4.4	5.9	7.3	8.8	10.3	11.8	13.3	14.8	16.3	17.8	70.0
70.5	0.0	1.5	3.0	4.5	6.0	7.5	9.0	10.5	12.1	13.6	15.1	16.7	18.2	70.5
71.0	0.0	1.5	3.1	4.6	6.2	7.7	9.3	10.8	12.4	13.9	15.5	17.1	18.7	71.0
71.5	0.0	1.6	3.2	4.7	6.3	7.9	9.5	11.1	12.7	14.3	15.9	17.6	19.2	71.5
72.0	0.0	1.6	3.2	4.9	6.5	8.1	9.8	11.4	13.0	14.7	16.4	18.1	19.8	72.0
72.5	0.0	1.7	3.3	5.0	6.7	8.3	10.0	11.7	13.4	15.1	16.8	18.6	20.3	72.5
73.0	0.0	1.7	3.4	5.1	6.9	8.6	10.3	12.1	13.8	15.6	17.3	19.1	20.9	73.0
73.5	0.0	1.8	3.5	5.3	7.1	8.8	10.6	12.4	14.2	16.0	17.9	19.7	21.6	73.5
74.0	0.0	1.8	3.6	5.4	7.3	9.1	10.9	12.8	14.7	16.5	18.4	20.3	22.3	74.0
74.5	0.0	1.9	3.7	5.6	7.5	9.4	11.3	13.2	15.1	17.1	19.0	21.0	23.0	74.5
75.0	0.0	1.9	3.9	5.8	7.7	9.7	11.7	13.6	15.6	17.6	19.7	21.7	23.8	75.0
75.5	0.0	2.0	4.0	6.0	8.0	10.0	12.1	14.1	16.2	18.3	20.4	22.5	24.7	75.5
76.0	0.0	2.1	4.1	6.2	8.3	10.4	12.5	14.6	16.8	18.9	21.1	23.3	25.6	76.0
76.5	0.0	2.1	4.3	6.4	8.6	10.8	13.0	15.2	17.4	19.6	21.9	24.2	26.6	76.5
77.0	0.0	2.2	4.4	6.7	8.9	11.2	13.5	15.7	18.1	20.4	22.8	25.2	27.7	77.0

KMA COMPASS CORRECTOR

DEC.	0°	1°	2°	3°	4°	5°	6°	7°	8°	9°	10°	11°	12°	13°	14°	15°	16°	17°	18°	19°	20°	21°	22°	23°
N	MARCH									APRIL									MAY				JUNE	
	21	23	26	28	31	3	5	8	11	13	16	19	22	25	28	1	5	8	12	16	21	26	1	10
	SEPTEMBER									AUGUST										JULY				
	23	21	18	16	13	10	8	5	2	30	28	25	22	19	16	12	9	5	2	28	24	19	12	3
S	SEPTEMBER									OCTOBER									NOVEMBER				DEC	
	23	26*	28	1	4	6	9	11	14	17	19	22	25	28	31	3	6	10	14	17	22	27	3	11
	MARCH									FEBRUARY									JANUARY					
	21	18	16	13	11	8	6	3	1	26	23	20	18	15	12	9	5	2	29	25	21	16	10	2

APPENDIX II   TABLE 27

Amplitudes

Latitude	Declination													Latitude
	6°0	6°5	7°0	7°5	8°0	8°5	9°0	9°5	10°0	10°5	11°0	11°5	12°0	
°	°	°	°	°	°	°	°	°	°	°	°	°	°	°
0	6.0	6.5	7.0	7.5	8.0	8.5	9.0	9.5	10.0	10.5	11.0	11.5	12.0	0
10	6.1	6.6	7.1	7.6	8.1	8.6	9.1	9.6	10.2	10.7	11.2	11.7	12.2	10
15	6.2	6.7	7.2	7.8	8.3	8.8	9.3	9.8	10.4	10.9	11.4	11.9	12.4	15
20	6.4	6.9	7.5	8.0	8.5	9.0	9.6	10.1	10.6	11.2	11.7	12.2	12.8	20
25	6.6	7.2	7.7	8.3	8.8	9.4	9.9	10.5	11.0	11.6	12.2	12.7	13.3	25
30	6.9	7.5	8.1	8.7	9.2	9.8	10.4	11.0	11.6	12.1	12.7	13.3	13.9	30
32	7.1	7.7	8.3	8.9	9.4	10.0	10.6	11.2	11.8	12.4	13.0	13.6	14.2	32
34	7.2	7.8	8.5	9.1	9.7	10.3	10.9	11.5	12.1	12.7	13.3	13.9	14.5	34
36	7.4	8.0	8.7	9.3	9.9	10.5	11.1	11.8	12.4	13.0	13.6	14.3	14.9	36
38	7.6	8.3	8.9	9.5	10.2	10.8	11.5	12.1	12.7	13.4	14.0	14.7	15.3	38
40	7.8	8.5	9.2	9.8	10.5	11.1	11.8	12.4	13.1	13.8	14.4	15.1	15.7	40
42	8.1	8.8	9.4	10.1	10.8	11.5	12.1	12.8	13.5	14.2	14.9	15.6	16.2	42
44	8.4	9.1	9.8	10.5	11.2	11.9	12.6	13.3	14.0	14.7	15.4	16.1	16.8	44
46	8.7	9.4	10.1	10.8	11.6	12.3	13.0	13.7	14.5	15.2	15.9	16.7	17.4	46
48	9.0	9.7	10.5	11.2	12.0	12.8	13.5	14.3	15.0	15.8	16.6	17.3	18.1	48
50	9.4	10.1	10.9	11.7	12.5	13.3	14.1	14.9	15.7	16.5	17.3	18.1	18.9	50
51	9.6	10.4	11.2	12.0	12.8	13.6	14.4	15.2	16.0	16.8	17.7	18.5	19.3	51
52	9.8	10.6	11.4	12.2	13.1	13.9	14.7	15.6	16.4	17.2	18.1	18.9	19.7	52
53	10.0	10.8	11.7	12.5	13.4	14.2	15.1	15.9	16.8	17.6	18.5	19.3	20.2	53
54	10.2	11.1	12.0	12.8	13.7	14.6	15.4	16.3	17.2	18.1	18.9	19.8	20.7	54
55	10.5	11.4	12.3	13.2	14.0	14.9	15.8	16.7	17.6	18.5	19.4	20.3	21.3	55
56	10.8	11.7	12.6	13.5	14.4	15.3	16.2	17.2	18.1	19.0	20.0	20.9	21.8	56
57	11.1	12.0	12.9	13.9	14.8	15.7	16.7	17.6	18.6	19.6	20.5	21.5	22.4	57
58	11.4	12.3	13.3	14.3	15.2	16.2	17.2	18.1	19.1	20.1	21.1	22.1	23.1	58
59	11.7	12.7	13.7	14.7	15.7	16.7	17.7	18.7	19.7	20.7	21.7	22.8	23.8	59
60	12.1	13.1	14.1	15.1	16.2	17.2	18.2	19.3	20.3	21.4	22.4	23.5	24.6	60
61	12.5	13.5	14.6	15.6	16.7	17.8	18.8	19.9	21.0	22.1	23.2	24.3	25.4	61
62	12.9	14.0	15.0	16.1	17.2	18.4	19.5	20.6	21.7	22.8	24.0	25.1	26.3	62
63	13.3	14.4	15.6	16.7	17.9	19.0	20.2	21.3	22.5	23.7	24.9	26.0	27.3	63
64	13.8	15.0	16.2	17.3	18.5	19.7	20.9	22.1	23.3	24.6	25.8	27.1	28.3	64
65.0	14.3	15.5	16.8	18.0	19.2	20.5	21.7	23.0	24.3	25.5	26.8	28.1	29.5	65.0
65.5	14.6	15.8	17.1	18.3	19.6	20.9	22.2	23.5	24.8	26.1	27.4	28.7	30.1	65.5
66.0	14.9	16.2	17.4	18.7	20.0	21.3	22.6	23.9	25.3	26.6	28.0	29.4	30.7	66.0
66.5	15.2	16.5	17.8	19.1	20.4	21.8	23.1	24.5	25.8	27.2	28.6	30.0	31.4	66.5
67.0	15.5	16.8	18.2	19.5	20.9	22.2	23.6	25.0	26.4	27.8	29.2	30.7	32.1	67.0
67.5	15.9	17.2	18.6	19.9	21.3	22.7	24.1	25.5	27.0	28.4	29.9	31.4	32.9	67.5
68.0	16.2	17.6	19.0	20.4	21.8	23.2	24.7	26.1	27.6	29.1	30.6	32.2	33.7	68.0
68.5	16.6	18.0	19.4	20.9	22.3	23.8	25.3	26.8	28.3	29.8	31.4	33.0	34.6	68.5
69.0	17.0	18.4	19.9	21.4	22.9	24.4	25.9	27.4	29.0	30.6	32.2	33.8	35.5	69.0
69.5	17.4	18.9	20.4	21.9	23.4	25.0	26.5	28.1	29.7	31.4	33.0	34.7	36.4	69.5
70.0	17.8	19.3	20.9	22.4	24.0	25.6	27.2	28.9	30.5	32.2	33.9	35.7	37.4	70.0
70.5	18.2	19.8	21.4	23.0	24.6	26.3	27.9	29.6	31.3	33.1	34.9	36.7	38.5	70.5
71.0	18.7	20.3	22.0	23.6	25.3	27.0	28.7	30.5	32.2	34.0	35.9	37.8	39.7	71.0
71.5	19.2	20.9	22.6	24.3	26.0	27.8	29.5	31.3	33.2	35.1	37.0	38.9	40.9	71.5
72.0	19.8	21.5	23.2	25.0	26.8	28.6	30.4	32.3	34.2	36.1	38.1	40.2	42.3	72.0
72.5	20.3	22.1	23.9	25.7	27.6	29.4	31.3	33.3	35.3	37.3	39.4	41.5	43.7	72.5
73.0	20.9	22.8	24.6	26.5	28.4	30.3	32.3	34.4	36.4	38.6	40.7	43.0	45.3	73.0
73.5	21.6	23.5	25.4	27.4	29.3	31.4	33.4	35.5	37.7	39.9	42.2	44.6	47.1	73.5
74.0	22.3	24.2	26.2	28.3	30.3	32.4	34.6	36.8	39.0	41.4	43.8	46.3	49.0	74.0
74.5	23.0	25.1	27.1	29.3	31.4	33.6	35.8	38.1	40.5	43.0	45.6	48.2	51.1	74.5
75.0	23.8	25.9	28.1	30.3	32.5	34.8	37.2	39.6	42.1	44.8	47.5	50.4	53.4	75.0
75.5	24.7	26.9	29.1	31.4	33.8	36.2	38.7	41.2	43.9	46.7	49.6	52.8	56.1	75.5
76.0	25.6	27.9	30.2	32.7	35.1	37.7	40.3	43.0	45.9	48.9	52.1	55.5	59.3	76.0
76.5	26.6	29.0	31.5	34.0	36.6	39.3	42.1	45.0	48.1	51.3	54.8	58.7	63.0	76.5
77.0	27.7	30.2	32.8	35.5	38.2	41.1	44.1	47.2	50.5	54.1	58.0	62.4	67.6	77.0

DEC.	0°	1°	2°	3°	4°	5°	6°	7°	8°	9°	10°	11°	12°	13°	14°	15°	16°	17°	18°	19°	20°	21°	22°	23°
N	MARCH									APRIL									MAY				JUNE	
	21	23	26	28	31	3	5	8	11	13	16	19	22	25	28	1	5	8	12	16	21	26	1	10
	SEPTEMBER									AUGUST									JULY					
	23	21	18	16	13	10	8	5	2	30	28	25	22	19	16	12	9	5	2	28	24	19	12	3
S	SEPTEMBER			OCTOBER												NOVEMBER							DEC	
	23	26°	28	1	4	6	9	11	14	17	19	22	25	28	31	3	6	10	14	17	22	27	3	11
	MARCH									FEBRUARY									JANUARY					
	21	18	16	13	11	8	6	3	1	26	23	20	18	15	12	9	5	2	29	25	21	16	10	2

APPENDIX II TABLE 27

Amplitudes

Latitude	12°0	12°5	13°0	13°5	14°0	14°5	15°0	15°5	16°0	16°5	17°0	17°5	18°0	Latitude
°	°	°	°	°	°	°	°	°	°	°	°	°	°	°
0	12. 0	12. 5	13. 0	13. 5	14. 0	14. 5	15. 0	15. 5	16. 0	16. 5	17. 0	17. 5	18. 0	0
10	12. 2	12. 7	13. 2	13. 7	14. 2	14. 7	15. 2	15. 7	16. 3	16. 8	17. 3	17. 8	18. 3	10
15	12. 4	12. 9	13. 5	14. 0	14. 5	15. 0	15. 5	16. 1	16. 6	17. 1	17. 6	18. 1	18. 7	15
20	12. 8	13. 3	13. 9	14. 4	14. 9	15. 5	16. 0	16. 5	17. 1	17. 6	18. 1	18. 7	19. 2	20
25	13. 3	13. 8	14. 4	14. 9	15. 5	16. 0	16. 6	17. 1	17. 7	18. 3	18. 8	19. 4	19. 9	25
30	13. 9	14. 5	15. 1	15. 6	16. 2	16. 8	17. 4	18. 0	18. 6	19. 1	19. 7	20. 3	20. 9	30
32	14. 2	14. 8	15. 4	16. 0	16. 6	17. 2	17. 8	18. 4	19. 0	19. 6	20. 2	20. 8	21. 4	32
34	14. 5	15. 1	15. 7	16. 4	17. 0	17. 6	18. 2	18. 8	19. 4	20. 0	20. 7	21. 3	21. 9	34
36	14. 9	15. 5	16. 1	16. 8	17. 4	18. 0	18. 7	19. 3	19. 9	20. 6	21. 2	21. 8	22. 5	36
38	15. 3	15. 9	16. 6	17. 2	17. 9	18. 5	19. 2	19. 8	20. 5	21. 1	21. 8	22. 4	23. 1	38
40	15. 7	16. 4	17. 1	17. 7	18. 4	19. 1	19. 7	20. 4	21. 1	21. 8	22. 4	23. 1	23. 8	40
41	16. 0	16. 7	17. 3	18. 0	18. 7	19. 4	20. 1	20. 8	21. 4	22. 1	22. 8	23. 5	24. 2	41
42	16. 2	16. 9	17. 6	18. 3	19. 0	19. 7	20. 4	21. 1	21. 8	22. 5	23. 2	23. 9	24. 6	42
43	16. 5	17. 2	17. 9	18. 6	19. 3	20. 0	20. 7	21. 4	22. 1	22. 9	23. 6	24. 3	25. 0	43
44	16. 8	17. 5	18. 2	18. 9	19. 7	20. 4	21. 1	21. 8	22. 5	23. 3	24. 0	24. 7	25. 4	44
45	17. 1	17. 8	18. 5	19. 3	20. 0	20. 7	21. 5	22. 2	22. 9	23. 7	24. 4	25. 2	25. 9	45
46	17. 4	18. 2	18. 9	19. 6	20. 4	21. 1	21. 9	22. 6	23. 4	24. 1	24. 9	25. 7	26. 4	46
47	17. 7	18. 5	19. 3	20. 0	20. 8	21. 5	22. 3	23. 1	23. 8	24. 6	25. 4	26. 2	26. 9	47
48	18. 1	18. 9	19. 6	20. 4	21. 2	22. 0	22. 8	23. 5	24. 3	25. 1	25. 9	26. 7	27. 5	48
49	18. 5	19. 3	20. 1	20. 8	21. 6	22. 4	23. 2	24. 0	24. 8	25. 7	26. 5	27. 3	28. 1	49
50	18. 9	19. 7	20. 5	21. 3	22. 1	22. 9	23. 7	24. 6	25. 4	26. 2	27. 1	27. 9	28. 7	50
51	19. 3	20. 1	20. 9	21. 8	22. 6	23. 4	24. 3	25. 1	26. 0	26. 8	27. 7	28. 5	29. 4	51
52	19. 7	20. 6	21. 4	22. 3	23. 1	24. 0	24. 9	25. 7	26. 6	27. 5	28. 3	29. 2	30. 1	52
53	20. 2	21. 1	21. 9	22. 8	23. 7	24. 6	25. 5	26. 4	27. 3	28. 2	29. 1	30. 0	30. 9	53
54	20. 7	21. 6	22. 5	23. 4	24. 3	25. 2	26. 1	27. 0	28. 0	28. 9	29. 8	30. 8	31. 7	54
55	21. 3	22. 2	23. 1	24. 0	24. 9	25. 9	26. 8	27. 8	28. 7	29. 7	30. 6	31. 6	32. 6	55
56	21. 8	22. 8	23. 7	24. 7	25. 6	26. 6	27. 6	28. 5	29. 5	30. 5	31. 5	32. 5	33. 5	56
57	22. 4	23. 4	24. 4	25. 4	26. 4	27. 4	28. 4	29. 4	30. 4	31. 4	32. 5	33. 5	34. 6	57
58	23. 1	24. 1	25. 1	26. 1	27. 2	28. 2	29. 2	30. 3	31. 3	32. 4	33. 5	34. 6	35. 7	58
59	23. 8	24. 8	25. 9	27. 0	28. 0	29. 1	30. 2	31. 3	32. 4	33. 5	34. 6	35. 7	36. 9	59
60	24. 6	25. 7	26. 7	27. 8	28. 9	30. 1	31. 2	32. 3	33. 5	34. 6	35. 8	37. 0	38. 2	60
61	25. 4	26. 5	27. 6	28. 8	29. 9	31. 1	32. 3	33. 5	34. 6	35. 9	37. 1	38. 3	39. 6	61
62	26. 3	27. 5	28. 6	29. 8	31. 0	32. 2	33. 5	34. 7	36. 0	37. 2	38. 5	39. 8	41. 2	62
63	27. 3	28. 5	29. 7	30. 9	32. 2	33. 5	34. 8	36. 1	37. 4	38. 7	40. 1	41. 5	42. 9	63
64	28. 3	29. 6	30. 9	32. 2	33. 5	34. 8	36. 2	37. 6	39. 0	40. 4	41. 8	43. 3	44. 8	64
65. 0	29. 5	30. 8	32. 2	33. 5	34. 9	36. 3	37. 8	39. 2	40. 7	42. 2	43. 8	45. 4	47. 0	65. 0
65. 5	30. 1	31. 5	32. 9	34. 3	35. 7	37. 1	38. 6	40. 1	41. 7	43. 2	44. 8	46. 5	48. 2	65. 5
66. 0	30. 7	32. 1	33. 6	35. 0	36. 5	38. 0	39. 5	41. 1	42. 7	44. 3	46. 0	47. 7	49. 4	66. 0
66. 5	31. 4	32. 9	34. 3	35. 8	37. 3	38. 9	40. 5	42. 1	43. 7	45. 4	47. 2	48. 9	50. 8	66. 5
67. 0	32. 1	33. 6	35. 1	36. 7	38. 3	39. 9	41. 5	43. 2	44. 9	46. 6	48. 4	50. 3	52. 3	67. 0
67. 5	32. 9	34. 4	36. 0	37. 6	39. 2	40. 9	42. 6	44. 3	46. 1	47. 9	49. 8	51. 8	53. 9	67. 5
68. 0	33. 7	35. 3	36. 9	38. 6	40. 2	41. 9	43. 7	45. 5	47. 4	49. 3	51. 3	53. 4	55. 6	68. 0
68. 5	34. 6	36. 2	37. 9	39. 6	41. 3	43. 1	44. 9	46. 8	48. 8	50. 8	52. 9	55. 1	57. 5	68. 5
69. 0	35. 5	37. 2	38. 9	40. 6	42. 5	44. 3	46. 2	48. 2	50. 3	52. 4	54. 7	57. 0	59. 6	69. 0
69. 5	36. 4	38. 2	40. 0	41. 8	43. 7	45. 6	47. 7	49. 7	51. 9	54. 2	56. 6	59. 2	61. 9	69. 5
70. 0	37. 4	39. 3	41. 1	43. 0	45. 0	47. 1	49. 2	51. 4	53. 7	56. 1	58. 7	61. 5	64. 6	70. 0
70. 5	38. 5	40. 4	42. 4	44. 4	46. 4	48. 6	50. 8	53. 2	55. 7	58. 3	61. 1	64. 3	67. 8	70. 5
71. 0	39. 7	41. 7	43. 8	45. 8	48. 0	50. 3	52. 7	55. 2	57. 8	60. 7	63. 9	67. 5	71. 7	71. 0
71. 5	40. 9	43. 0	45. 1	47. 4	49. 7	52. 1	54. 7	57. 4	60. 3	63. 5	67. 1	71. 4	76. 9	71. 5
72. 0	42. 3	44. 5	46. 7	49. 1	51. 5	54. 1	56. 9	59. 9	63. 1	66. 8	71. 1	76. 7	90. 0	72. 0
72. 5	43. 7	46. 0	48. 4	50. 9	53. 6	56. 4	59. 4	62. 7	66. 4	70. 8	76. 5	90. 0		72. 5
73. 0	45. 3	47. 8	50. 3	53. 0	55. 8	58. 9	62. 3	66. 1	70. 5	76. 3	90. 0			73. 0
73. 5	47. 1	49. 6	52. 4	55. 3	58. 4	61. 8	65. 7	70. 2	76. 0	90. 0				73. 5
74. 0	49. 0	51. 7	54. 7	57. 9	61. 4	65. 3	69. 9	75. 8	90. 0					74. 0
74. 5	51. 1	54. 1	57. 3	60. 9	64. 9	69. 5	75. 6	90. 0						74. 5

KMA COMPASS CORRECTOR

DEC.	0°	1°	2°	3°	4°	5°	6°	7°	8°	9°	10°	11°	12°	13°	14°	15°	16°	17°	18°	19°	20°	21°	22°	23°
N	MARCH									APRIL									MAY				JUNE	
	21	23	26	28	31	3	5	8	11	13	16	19	22	25	28	1	5	8	12	16	21	26	1	10
	SEPTEMBER									AUGUST									JULY					
	23	21	18	16	13	10	8	5	2	30	28	25	22	19	16	12	9	5	2	28	24	19	12	3
S	SEPTEMBER			OCTOBER															NOVEMBER				DEC	
	23	26°	28	1	4	6	9	11	14	17	19	22	25	28	31	3	6	10	14	17	22	27	3	1
	MARCH									FEBRUARY									JANUARY					
	21	18	16	13	11	8	6	3	1	26	23	20	18	15	12	9	5	2	29	25	21	16	10	2

APPENDIX II   TABLE 27
Amplitudes

Latitude	18°0	18°5	19°0	19°5	20°0	20°5	21°0	21°5	22°0	22°5	23°0	23°5	24°0	Latitude
0	18.0	18.5	19.0	19.5	20.0	20.5	21.0	21.5	22.0	22.5	23.0	23.5	24.0	0
10	18.3	18.8	19.3	19.8	20.3	20.8	21.3	21.8	22.4	22.9	23.4	23.9	24.4	10
15	18.7	19.2	19.7	20.2	20.7	21.3	21.8	22.3	22.8	23.3	23.9	24.4	24.9	15
20	19.2	19.7	20.3	20.8	21.3	21.9	22.4	23.0	23.5	24.0	24.6	25.1	25.6	20
25	19.9	20.5	21.1	21.6	22.2	22.7	23.3	23.9	24.4	25.0	25.5	26.1	26.7	25
30	20.9	21.5	22.1	22.7	23.3	23.9	24.4	25.0	25.6	26.2	26.8	27.4	28.0	30
32	21.4	22.0	22.6	23.2	23.8	24.4	25.0	25.6	26.2	26.8	27.4	28.0	28.7	32
34	21.9	22.5	23.1	23.7	24.4	25.0	25.6	26.2	26.9	27.5	28.1	28.7	29.4	34
36	22.5	23.1	23.7	24.4	25.0	25.7	26.3	26.9	27.6	28.2	28.9	29.5	30.2	36
38	23.1	23.7	24.4	25.1	25.7	26.4	27.1	27.7	28.4	29.1	29.7	30.4	31.1	38
40	23.8	24.5	25.2	25.8	26.5	27.2	27.9	28.6	29.3	30.0	30.7	31.4	32.1	40
41	24.2	24.9	25.6	26.3	26.9	27.6	28.3	29.1	29.8	30.5	31.2	31.9	32.6	41
42	24.6	25.3	26.0	26.7	27.4	28.1	28.8	29.5	30.3	31.0	31.7	32.5	33.2	42
43	25.0	25.7	26.4	27.2	27.9	28.6	29.3	30.1	30.8	31.6	32.3	33.0	33.8	43
44	25.4	26.2	26.9	27.6	28.4	29.1	29.9	30.6	31.4	32.1	32.9	33.7	34.4	44
45	25.9	26.7	27.4	28.2	28.9	29.7	30.5	31.2	32.0	32.8	33.5	34.3	35.1	45
46	26.4	27.2	27.9	28.7	29.5	30.3	31.1	31.8	32.6	33.4	34.2	35.0	35.8	46
47	26.9	27.7	28.5	29.3	30.1	30.9	31.7	32.5	33.3	34.1	35.0	35.8	36.6	47
48	27.5	28.3	29.1	29.9	30.7	31.6	32.4	33.2	34.0	34.9	35.7	36.6	37.4	48
49	28.1	28.9	29.8	30.6	31.4	32.3	33.1	34.0	34.8	35.7	36.6	37.4	38.3	49
50	28.7	29.6	30.4	31.3	32.1	33.0	33.9	34.8	35.6	36.5	37.4	38.3	39.3	50
51	29.4	30.3	31.2	32.0	32.9	33.8	34.7	35.6	36.5	37.5	38.4	39.3	40.3	51
52	30.1	31.0	31.9	32.8	33.7	34.7	35.6	36.5	37.5	38.4	39.4	40.4	41.3	52
53	30.9	31.8	32.8	33.7	34.6	35.6	36.5	37.5	38.5	39.5	40.5	41.5	42.5	53
54	31.7	32.7	33.6	34.6	35.6	36.6	37.6	38.6	39.6	40.6	41.7	42.7	43.8	54
55	32.6	33.6	34.6	35.6	36.6	37.6	38.7	39.7	40.8	41.9	42.9	44.0	45.2	55
56	33.5	34.6	35.6	36.7	37.7	38.8	39.9	41.0	42.1	43.2	44.3	45.5	46.7	56
57	34.6	35.6	36.7	37.8	38.9	40.0	41.1	42.3	43.5	44.6	45.8	47.1	48.3	57
58	35.7	36.8	37.9	39.1	40.2	41.4	42.6	43.8	45.0	46.2	47.5	48.8	50.1	58
59	36.9	38.0	39.2	40.4	41.6	42.8	44.1	45.4	46.7	48.0	49.3	50.7	52.2	59
60.0	38.2	39.4	40.6	41.9	43.2	44.5	45.8	47.1	48.5	49.9	51.4	52.9	54.4	60.0
60.5	38.9	40.1	41.4	42.7	44.0	45.3	46.7	48.1	49.5	51.0	52.5	54.1	55.7	60.5
61.0	39.6	40.9	42.2	43.5	44.9	46.3	47.7	49.1	50.6	52.1	53.7	55.3	57.0	61.0
61.5	40.4	41.7	43.0	44.4	45.8	47.2	48.7	50.2	51.7	53.3	55.0	56.7	58.5	61.5
62.0	41.2	42.5	43.9	45.3	46.8	48.2	49.8	51.3	52.9	54.6	56.3	58.1	60.0	62.0
62.5	42.0	43.4	44.8	46.3	47.8	49.3	50.9	52.5	54.2	56.0	57.8	59.7	61.7	62.5
63.0	42.9	44.3	45.8	47.3	48.9	50.5	52.1	53.8	55.6	57.5	59.4	61.4	63.6	63.0
63.5	43.8	45.3	46.9	48.4	50.0	51.7	53.4	55.2	57.1	59.1	61.1	63.4	65.7	63.5
64.0	44.8	46.4	48.0	49.6	51.3	53.0	54.8	56.7	58.7	60.8	63.0	65.5	68.1	64.0
64.5	45.9	47.5	49.1	50.8	52.6	54.4	56.3	58.4	60.5	62.7	65.2	67.9	70.9	64.5
65.0	47.0	48.7	50.4	52.2	54.0	56.0	58.0	60.1	62.4	64.9	67.6	70.7	74.2	65.0
65.5	48.2	49.9	51.7	53.6	55.6	57.6	59.8	62.1	64.6	67.3	70.4	74.1	78.8	65.5
66.0	49.4	51.3	53.2	55.2	57.2	59.4	61.8	64.3	67.1	70.2	73.9	78.6	90.0	66.0
66.5	50.8	52.7	54.7	56.8	59.1	61.4	64.0	66.8	70.0	73.7	78.5	90.0		66.5
67.0	52.3	54.3	56.4	58.7	61.1	63.7	66.5	69.7	73.5	78.4	90.0			67.0
67.5	53.9	56.0	58.3	60.7	63.3	66.2	69.5	73.3	78.2	90.0				67.5
68.0	55.6	57.9	60.4	63.0	65.9	69.2	73.1	78.1	90.0					68.0
68.5	57.5	60.0	62.7	65.6	68.9	72.9	77.9	90.0						68.5
69.0	59.6	62.3	65.3	68.7	72.6	77.7	90.0							69.0
69.5	61.9	65.0	68.4	72.4	77.6	90.0								69.5
70.0	64.6	68.1	72.2	77.4	90.0									70.0
70.5	67.8	71.9	77.2	90.0										70.5
71.0	71.7	77.1	90.0											71.0
71.5	76.9	90.0												71.5
72.0	90.0													72.0

Index

Adjusting the compass, 5,
    16, 35–39
Ahab, Captain, 3, 7
Altitude, 26–27
Amplitude 6, 22, 23–24,
    49, 55, 57, 59, 61, 63
Anneal, 36
Annual change, 11
Annual decrease, 10
Annual increase, 10
Armchair Sailor, 46
Athwartship magnets (C
    magnets), 38–39
Azimuth, 5, 21, 37, 43

B magnets, 37–39
Baker Lyman and Co., 46
Bearings, 19–21, 26–27,
    32, 36–37, 42
Bearings, jeweled, 13
Big Dipper, 24–26, 28
Binnacle, ix, 5, 37
Blue pole, 8
Bluewater Books and
    Charts, 47
*Bowditch Publication No.
    9,* 24, 43, 49

Brass fittings, 37
Bubbles, 36
Bulkheads, 13

C magnets, 38–39
Calculator, 24, 47
CAN DEAD MEN VOTE
    TWICE, 17
Cardinal magnetic
    heading, 38
Cassiopeia, 26–28
Celestaire, Inc., 47
Celestial body, 21
Centerline, 11, 20
Change of course, 13
Chart table, 32
Charts, 1, 9, 10, 20–21, 45
Compass, ix, 3, 4, 5, 9, 11,
    13, 14, 15, 20, 31–32,
    35, 37, 39
Compass adjusters, 16, 20
Compass bearing (PSCØ),
    19, 32–33
Compass card, 8, 13, 14,
    42
Compass correction,
    23–30, 45

Compass correction card, 33
Compass Corrector, 23, 25, 42, 56, 58, 60, 62
Compass course, 16
Compass Deviation Card, 11, 32, 36
Compass error, 3–6, 9–14, 15–17, 19–21, 26, 31–33
Compass heading (PSC), 10, 16–18, 20, 32–33
Compass light, 14
Compass north, 10, 16
Compass rose, 10, 11, 20
Compensating magnets, 13, 37
Compounds, mastic, 37
Constant heading, 14
Constellations, 24–25
Cook, Captain James, 1
Correcting the compass, 16–17
Correction, 9, 27, 30
Correctors, 38
Cosine, 24
Courses, 31, 36

Date, 22, 24–25, 51–53
Dawn, 26
Dead reckoning, 6
Declination, 24–25, 37, 49, 51–53, 55–63
Defense Mapping Agency (DMAHTC), 42–43

Degaussing systems, 41–42
Demagnetization, 13
Depth finder, 16
Deviation, 5, 10, 11, 16–18, 31, 32–33, 35, 37–38
Deviation magnets, 39
Deviation Table, 31–33, 38
Dip (height of eye), 27–30
Direct current, 14
Dummy compass, 20, 37, 47
Dusk, 26

E, 10, 16
East, 39
East point, 24
East-west headings, 21, 37
Electrical, 13
Electrical cables, 4, 6, 13
Electrical equipment, 14, 35
Electronic equipment, 10, 14, 35
Equator, 3, 26
Error, 9, 10, 13, 14, 21, 31

Filling plug, 36
Flinders bars, 41
Fore-and-aft magnets (B magnets), 37–39
Friction, 13
Frozen compass, 13–14, 37

Geographic meridian, 10
Geographic poles, 10
Global Positioning System (GPS), 6
Grain alcohol, 36
Greenwich Hour Angle (GHA), 51–53
Gyro compasses, 4, 5
Gyro, 6

Headings, 10, 13–14, 21, 31–32, 36–37
Heeling magnets, 41
Height of Eye, 27–30
Helm, 32
Helmsman, 4, 11
Hemispheres, 4
Horizon, 24–26

Intercardinal heading, 38
Intermittent deviation, 14
Interpolating, 35–36
Inverted magnets, 3–4

Kelvin Hughes, 48
Kerosene, 36
KMA Compass Corrector, 23, 25, 42, 56, 58, 60, 62

Landfall, 6, 15, 19
Latitude, 22, 24–27, 37, 41, 55, 57, 59, 61, 63
Lazy compass, 13–14
Lifeboat compass, 7
Lightning, 3

Long-Term Almanac, 49, 51–53, 55
Lubber's line, 11, 20

Magnetic compass, 4, 7–8
Magnetic field, 5
Magnetic forces, 10, 14
Magnetic headings, 10, 16–18, 38
Magnetic meridian, 8, 10
Magnetic north, 8, 10
Magnetic poles, 8, 10
Magnetic variation, 10, 12
Magnetic variation chart, 12
Magnetization, 7, 8
Magnets, 3, 8, 39
Mechanical wear, 13
Micronesia, 1
Misalignment, 11, 13
Moby Dick, 3
Moon, 21, 26

Nautical Almanac, 21, 43, 47
Navigation, 1, 8
Navigation tables, 21
Navigational instruments, 8, 45
Navigator, 6, 45
Navy compass, 20
Needles, 3, 7–8
North, 39
North magnetic pole (Blue pole), 8

North Star, 21, 23, 24,
26–28, 37, 41
North-South headings, 21,
38
Northern hemisphere, 21,
37

Observed altitude (Ho), 27
Oscillation, 13, 14, 35

Pelorus, 20, 37, 47
Pequod, 3, 6
Planets, 21
Plotting position, 19
Plotting sheet, 20
Pointers, 26–28
Polaris, 21, 23, 24, 26–28,
37, 41
Polarity, 3–4
Polynesia, 1
Port, 39
PSC heading (per standard
compass), 32–33
PSC Ø (per standard
compass bearing),
32–33
Publication 226, 12, 18,
43
Publication 229, 21, 43
Publication 249, 21, 43
Publication 260, 21, 37,
43

Quadrantal correctors, ix,
36

Quick and Easy Compass
Corrector, 23, 25, 42,
56, 58, 60, 62
Quick and Easy Skyclock,
24, 26–30, 41

Radar, 4
Radiotelephone, 16
"Red" *Azimuth Tables,*
21, 37, 43
Red pole, 8
Relative bearings, 20
Remote-reading compass,
14
Ritchie, E.S. & Sons Inc.,
ix
Ruler, 20

Screwdriver, 37
Screws, 37
Sextant altitude (Hs), 26,
27, 30
Sextant observations, 24,
26–27, 41
Sextants, 47
Short-wave radio, 47
Sight Reduction Tables, 43
Sight vane, 20
Sights, 27
Sine, 24
Skyclock, 24, 26–30, 41
South, 34
South magnetic pole (Red
pole), 8
Spheres, ix, 36

Spherical compass, 20
Starboard, 39
Stars, 21, 27
Steel vessels, ix, 13, 35
Steering, 19, 42
Sun, 6, 21, 22, 23–24, 37, 49, 51
Swinging ship, 5, 31–33, 37–38

TIMID VIRGINS MAKE DULL COMPANIONS, 17
Tools, 37
True bearing (True Ø), 9, 21, 24, 32–33
True compass courses, 9
True course, 5, 16

True heading, 16–18
True north, 10, 16

Uncorrecting the compass, 16–17
Ursa Major, 24, 26–28

Variation, 10–11, 16–18, 32–33

W, 10, 16
Water, 7, 36
Weak magnets, 13–14
West, 39
West point, 24
Wind rose, 8
Wood alcohol, 36

Other titles of interest

Marine Salvage: A Guide for Boaters and Divers
by George H. Reid

All aspects of refloating stranded vessels, salvaging sinking or sunken vessels, conducting rescue tows, and recovering submerged objects or material are addressed in detail.

Basic Coastal Navigation
by Frank J. Larkin

A clearly written, easy to understand introduction to coastal navigation, outlining most of the techniques of piloting fundamental to safe navigation, even with today's electronic aids.

The Marine Electrical and Electronics Bible
by John C. Payne

The author has put together a concise, useful, and thoroughly practical guide explaining in detail how to select, install, maintain, and troubleshoot all the electrical and electronic systems on a boat.

Metal Boats
by Ken Scott

This comprehensive guide is a must for those planning to buy a metal boat, complete a boat from a bare hull, or build a completely new steel or aluminum boat themselves.

Understanding Weatherfax
by Mike Harris

This book provides the essentials needed to set up a weatherfax receiver and derive useful forecast information from the results.

Using GPS
by Conrad Dixon

This book will help owners get the best from their sets and make full use of the facilities available, whether simply position fixing and course setting or interfacing with radar, Loran, autopilots, knotmeters, chart plotters, or video sounders.

Sheridan House
America's Favorite Sailing Books